Parent-Teen Bonding & Faith Collection

Parenting Teens Through Faith + Inspirational 30-Day Affirmation Challenge for Teens

by

Scriptseeds

© Copyright 2022 by Scriptseeds- All rights reserved.

The content contained within this book may not be reproduced, duplicated or transmitted without direct written permission from the author or the publisher.

Under no circumstances will any blame or legal responsibility be held against the publisher, or author, for any damages, reparation, or monetary loss due to the information contained within this book. Either directly or indirectly. You are responsible for your own choices, actions, and results.

Legal Notice:

This book is copyright protected. This book is only for personal use. You cannot amend, distribute, sell, use, quote or paraphrase any part, or the content within this book, without the consent of the author or publisher.

Disclaimer Notice:

Please note the information contained within this document is for educational and entertainment purposes only. All effort has been executed to present accurate, up to date, and reliable, complete information. No warranties of any kind are declared or implied. Readers acknowledge that the author is not engaging in the rendering of legal, financial, medical or professional advice. The content within this book has been derived from various sources. Please consult a licensed professional before attempting any techniques outlined in this book.

By reading this document, the reader agrees that under no circumstances is the author responsible for any losses, direct or indirect, which are incurred as a result of the use of the information contained within this document, including, but not limited to, — errors, omissions, or inaccuracies.

CONTENTS

Introduction	1
1. Relationship Goals	5
2. The Real Adversary	15
3. Intrusive Technology	23
4. Intrusive Media and Culture	34
5. Intrusion in Education	41
6. Mind, Body and Spirit	49
7. Virtuous Attributes	64
8. Conclusion	73
Introduction	78
Dedication	81
Day 1	82
Day 2	84
Day 3	86
Day 4	88
Day 5	90
Day 6	92
Day 7	94
Day 8	96
Day 9	98
Day 10	100

Day 11	102
Day 12	104
Day 13	106
Day 14	108
Day 15	110
Day 16	112
Day 17	114
Day 18	116
Day 19	118
Day 20	120
Day 21	122
Day 22	124
Day 23	126
Day 24	128
Day 25	130
Day 26	132
Day 27	134
Day 28	136
Day 29	138
Day 30	140
Conclusion	142
Resources Book 1	145
Resources Book 2	155

Parenting Teens Through Faith

7 Steps to an Improved Parent-Teen Relationship

Boost Your Teen's Confidence & Mental Strength to Withstand Negative Influences, Bullies and School Pressure

by

Scriptseeds

Introduction

"I want to go to Kelly's birthday party tomorrow."

"Oh, is it at her house? What time is it?"

"It is an all-night party at her house."

"All-night party?!!"

"Yeah. Everyone from school will be there!"

"You are too young for an all-night party; I can't allow you to go."

"Mom!! All my friends from school are going, and Kelly's parents organized the party for her."

"Even if all your friends are going, I do not agree with you going to an all-night party."

"I knew you wouldn't allow me. You never allow me to do anything fun. Kelly's parents organized the party to make her happy; you will never do something like that for me!!"

"Listen, stop raising your voice at me. Any more disrespectful words from you, and you will be grounded for the week!"

"I hate you!! I hate you!!! You never let me do anything fun!!! I hate you!!"

It seems unfair to give 100% effort physically, emotionally, and financially of yourself toward raising your child and still be disrespected by your teen. They pull away emotionally, care less about your opinions, and only seem to care about themselves and their friends. You may feel as though you are losing influence over them and fighting for their attention. It's hard to keep your faith strong, let alone instill godly faith in them. If you're finding yourself feeling afraid or hopeless, chin up. It's time to take back control, learn how to stand up to intrusive influences, use God-given authority to protect and guide your teen and strengthen your bond with your teen. The first step on that journey is to stop thinking about yourself as a powerless parent and tap into God's strength and love, which will provide you with all the patience and wisdom you need.

You'll need that strength and patience to confront all the influences that surround your child. Teenagers nowadays are exposed to dozens of different threats, from drugs, violence, and predators to cyber-bullying and a toxic culture of violent and explicit content. Most of the media, music, and TV programs that target teenage audiences are sexually suggestive, superficial, and, in many ways, designed to belittle teens' self-image and persuade them to consume the advertised products to feel accepted and relevant. All these influences may seem harmless on the surface, but they can create an environment where children feel like there's something wrong with them if they don't conform to society's expectations of what makes someone "normal." Your teen might also fear that they'll never make any friends if they don't succumb to peer pressure, and they might start to feel torn between the values taught at home and those promoted in popular culture. Your child could quickly suffer from depression, anxiety, or eating disorders if they don't have proper guidance. All that said, parents can't keep their teens sheltered every day. At the same time, it's exhausting and stressful to constantly keep up with where they are and what they're doing at every moment of the day. This book will allow you to understand the potential impacts of these influences on their hearts and minds and how to respond to them. Pray as you read and ask God to show you how to see the toxic nature of external influences, how your teen's heart and mind are vulnerable, and how He can help you and your teen find the path of abundant life. If you have more than one child, ask God to give you direction with each one individually and be prepared to adjust and accommodate to their personalities. God made each of them unique in that they learn and respond uniquely.

Teenagers struggle so much because this shiny culture seemingly promoting positive values has subliminal, destructive messages lurking beneath the surface. Don't be mistaken—you are fighting a spiritual war for your child's future and well-being. Modern culture aims to make them weak. It wants to turn them into mindless, meek consumers and prevent them from thinking critically and choosing to act on their moral convictions rather than self-indulgence. To quote John Wesley: "As the most dangerous winds may enter at little openings, so the devil never enters more dangerously than by little unobserved incidents, which seem to be nothing, yet insensibly open the heart to great temptations" (1766).

To get the most out of this book the reader must strive to have an open receptive heart and mind. Be willing to see that no one is perfect and good except Jesus Christ and His Father who sent Him to us. Also understand that despite our mistakes, God has more than enough grace to meet us where we are, pick us back up and restore love, peace, and healing in our family, no matter how broken and dysfunctional it may seem. Better parenting starts with self-reflection. Naturally for most children, everything revolves around self-fulfillment and they struggle to care about anything beyond their immediate needs and pleasures. Oh but so do we! As adults, our lives may sometimes feel empty and shallow, even with comfortable homes, the latest clothing, cars and gadgets. Self-indulgence is one of the most destructive philosophies of the modern era. It appears people fail to realize that God created us to live for Him and in harmony with each other as we serve each other. Instead, many prefer to live for their gain and interests above anything or anyone else. Why is that?

It is because the condition of humanity changed when Adam and Eve chose to disobey God in Genesis of the Bible that we all struggle in a life separated from God. Humans became estranged from the Creator, naturally began to think sinfully, and became drawn toward darkness. Because God is loving, He gave humans free will, which is the ability to make our own choices within our human abilities, of course. Ever since the account of Adam and Eve, we have lived in a fallen world, but the result is that we are all born sinners and must be held accountable for our choices, just like Adam and Eve. With the gap between ourselves and God, we may feel a large void, viewing life as meaningless at times, seeking the perfect house, furnishings, achievements, profits, and popularity. Even after attaining these goals, we would still need something else. Religion is not the answer. Even the devil has a religion. There are so many religious people who are far from God and don't know Jesus. The missing key is a relationship with God, with Jesus. Parents and guardians, there is no better time than now to reconnect with your heavenly Father, trust in Him and strengthen your faith first.

Strengthening your faith in God is like putting your spiritual life-saving oxygen mask on. This positions you to help your child. Children are a gift from God, and you're the best-qualified person to guide, nurture, and raise your teen to live the life God intends for them. Your teenager might seem rebellious. They might look like they're avoiding you and don't need you anymore; worse, say they hate you. But inside, they're still a child, longing for love, encouragement, and guidance to overcome daily attacks on their body, mind, and spirit. Be it the things they pick up at school, drugs, violence, and obscenity that lurks at every corner when your child is out with their friends; you're fighting a single enemy. Let's not give in to the fear of these influences but instead give attention, thoughts, and prayers to God and plead for wisdom and strength to walk through life with kindness, compassion, and the love of God in our hearts as we raise our teens. These attributes are what defeat the enemy. This book will show you how to navigate all sorts of toxic influences on your child and lead them to faith, guarding their minds to preserve their well-being. There's so much going on out there. It's impossible to control every action and decision your child makes. It can be overwhelming for any parent to keep up! It's a full-time job to arm ourselves and our teens with the right tools for victory. To do so, you need a plan. Prepare to establish a foundation of faith and foster relationships that form a barrier the enemy cannot break through. The Bible says, "For we do not wrestle against flesh and blood, but against the rulers, against the authorities, against the cosmic powers over this present darkness, against the spiritual forces of evil in the heavenly places" (New American Standard Version Bible, 2001, Ephesians 6:12). God is on your side. Trust Him to help you, and you'll be able to relax because, eventually, your teen will be better prepared to overcome obstacles and temptations and live out their best life possible with a transformed life in Christ.

1

RELATIONSHIP GOALS

Paula, a divorced single mother of a 16-year-old boy, Matthew, was so glad to be dating someone. She had been dating him for months on the weekends when Matthew was with his dad. One day she met up with her boyfriend on the weekend when Matthew was with her. Matthew was very hostile to his mother's boyfriend and didn't speak to either of them. Matthew was also very short with his mother and demonstrated a bad attitude for the next several days. Paula realized her son was insecure about losing time with his mother because of her boyfriend. She knew she needed to invest more in her relationship with her son, spend more one on one time with him, and have more conversations with him. Her goal was to reassure him that she would always be there for him, to listen to him, understand and love him.

The primary benefit of any good relationship is undivided attention from with whom you have the relationship, meaning your presence without anyone else, or any distractions, even if there's nothing to discuss. Talking about something together is great too when there are no interruptions and the other person is not just hearing but listening, empathizing, and understanding. An ideal parent-teen solid relationship does not just involve the two of you. It should be three – with God! In other words, when you communicate with your child, communicate as if Jesus is standing right there, the same Jesus who loves your child just as he loves you. Every child has unique personalities, experiences, desires, and learning styles, even twins! If you have more than one child, spending time alone with each one separately will allow you to know their personality traits, and each child will appreciate the individual one-on-one attention. They will also enjoy personal attention without comparison to their siblings or other children. It's helpful to be mindful of your voice tone, body language, and choice of words. Although it's easier said than done, your child will be much more receptive to what you are communicating when you speak with respect and love. It is possible to be angry, and rightfully so, when your child disobeys or disrespects you but having self-control as you speak with your parental authority will lead to a much better outcome. It's against our nature to speak carefully and calmly when our teens are emotional, triggering our emotions. Times like these are when we need to rely on God the most. If you have a solid relationship with God that makes you whole and complete, you can easily give more of yourself toward your relationship with your children. Let's discuss some other related goals.

God's design for the family unit is structured so that children have both a mother and a father. However, many families are increasingly lacking one of them. Children who grow up without a father tend to have a higher risk of crime and underachievement. A lack of paternal authority at home increases the risk of adverse outcomes such as lower academic achievement, a higher risk of dropping out of high school, and a higher risk of engaging in criminality and violent behaviors. They might also struggle to maintain healthy relationships with other people. Sadly, the percentage of children living without their parents has significantly increased since 1960. It has doubled in numbers, with between 17% and 33% of the overall teen boy population living without a father. If this is the case with your family, it would be in your best interest as well as your child's interest to consider finding a proper role model for your child. As recent new research has shown, boys need to have a male role model.

Now you must wonder, what are the circumstances for these boys living without a father? There's more than one way for a father to be absent from the family. In part, higher divorce rates produce more single mothers than before. However, there are also diseases causing the early deaths of fathers, as well as a preoccupation with work that may not allow fathers to be as involved with their children's lives as they should. A mother is generally a source of care and love. She is someone whom a child depends on for survival. Fathers, on the other hand, signify authority. Children take in paternal influences concerning competence and achievement, whether in school, chores, or career. Not having a father in their life is risky since it can deplete a child's desire to achieve, prove themselves, and do well.

Now, a mother has a more emotional impact on her children's psychology. The relationship with a mother affects how boys and girls communicate intimate feelings, how well they'll be able to navigate relationships, how much they'll trust the opposite gender and the quality of friendships and personal relationships they'll have.

As you can see, both parents provide complementary influences on their children. There's a prevailing view in psychology that children can't develop healthily unless the relationships with their parents are in balance. If a parent is absent, a child lacks the said parental influence.

When talking about absent parents, we most frequently talk about boys. Yet girls suffer, too, when they don't have adequate maternal and paternal influence. In fact, for a daughter, a father is a career-driving influence. Some psychologists explain that a fatherly presence allows daughters to connect psychologically with the powerful aspects of their personality and be more driven and courageous in life. Women who have close relationships with their fathers tend to have higher academic achievement, more rewarding careers, and fewer teen pregnancies. The more stable the household was, the stronger and better achieved the daughters were. They also had a lower risk of depression and were more satisfied with their appearance and lives.

If you are a single parent, foster a relationship between your child and the other parent. If the other parent cannot be in the child's life, consider finding a positive male or female role model for your child. For this, you can turn to coaches, church leaders, or your extended family members whom you know very well and trust. This guidance also applies if you are widowed. Whether male or female, an absent parent needs a surrogate of sorts so that the child can begin to build a connection with the role model of the missing gender.

Your teenager is rushing upstairs, slamming their door behind them. You just told them they couldn't have their friends over on a school night, and they've responded that it was their turn to return hospitality to friends who have previously invited them over. Although you agree, you note that they will undeniably stay up late and that the child won't have the time to prepare for their test tomorrow morning. You both have valid reasons and suggest arranging a get-together at a more suitable time, but that doesn't stop a tantrum. How can teenagers always aim for that one thing they can't get, no matter how many options you give them? Even if you do everything "by the book," it appears you can't accommodate your teen's request for the time being. They perhaps always seem to come up with one extra demand, something that's important to them but not an option for you. Staying calm seems like an impossible mission, and it takes all your reserve not to go after them and scold them into oblivion. We've all been there! But guess what? You are a team. A child and their parents are there to support each other's growth. You're not the only one doing the raising. "To raise" means to nurture growth and take a person, a plant, or an animal from a smaller to a more elevated level of being. Your child does that for you the same way you do it for them. A very important characteristic in a solid relationship is humility. It doesn't mean being weak. On the contrary, it's a strength because it takes strength to be humble instead of prideful. It may seem counterintuitive to be humble in your relationship with your teen, but the best leaders out there demonstrate humility, and you are leading your teen. You also want to live out characteristics you hope to model and pass on to your teen.

Your teenager is exercising their free will and independence. No matter how frustrating their rebellion seems, you'd appreciate their stamina in the face of peer pressure, so they don't forget everything they believe in and submit themselves to group mentality. If your teenager is to have any kind of critical thinking and nerve in life, well, you're the first person they'll exercise it on. That's how they get used to standing their ground. Still, it is necessary to preserve peace at home. Now, in the power struggle between you and the child, you're both trying to "save face." If you allow the struggle even to occur, it starts to feel like you must escalate just so you don't lose an argument, and your teenager is doing the same. No one wants to be humiliated and feel outwitted. So, what do you do?

As you ponder the kindest ways to discipline your child, you know a teenager is always at risk from inappropriate behaviors, substance abuse, and harmful influences, and that fear keeps you on edge. Your child, on the other hand, likely feels misunderstood. Perhaps they're doing their best, although sad and angry over making a mistake and letting you down. Bear in mind that teenagers still can't perceive the entirety of the risks surrounding them. They're shortsighted in that regard. If you asked an average teen whether it's suitable to hang out with troublesome peers, most would agree that there's no harm in it if they're acting the way they should. They can't anticipate that the wrong crowd can put them in dangerous situations or abuse their kindness.

To start with, understand where your teen is coming from. Put yourself in their shoes and try remembering what it felt like to be genuinely innocent, wishing to go about your day carelessly. Teenagers don't get that dinner won't cook itself, and they can't perceive how much labor goes into maintaining a comfortable, orderly life. To them, life unfolds like a movie in which they have some serious "plot armor." They feel like nothing wrong can happen to them and think so correctly since they move around in sheltered, protected environments. Domestic and school demands, in many ways, appear to them as nonsensical.

Now that you can understand where your child is coming from, perhaps you can tune in with the same humility. You have enormous power over your teenagers, so use that perception to humble yourself and be the bigger person in a power struggle. Aside from that, practice the following strategies to cultivate a stronger relationship with your child.

Trust that your child is hungry for your approval. They struggle to admit mistakes before you because they feel like doing so lets you down. Your child's anger comes from having childlike feelings that a teenager who aims to look like an adult doesn't want to admit. In a way, accepting an error for a teenager is like admitting defeat. They don't want to feel embarrassed in front of you, and they still don't understand what to do so that you're happy with their behavior and achievement. When a teenager is being spiteful, they avoid the humiliation of blame. The only way around that is to reframe mistakes, take out the blame, and replace it with accountability. Your teenager will most certainly struggle to take accountability no matter what you do, but at least they won't feel so profoundly oppressed that they're willing to disregard everything you taught them as soon as they leave the house.

Your child is getting angry at you because they are scared. They don't want to admit they're afraid, so they lash out at you. Other times, they'll lash out because they feel insecure. Being branded a "loser" by the conventional world is every teenager's worst fear, and teens who follow Christ are afraid of being targeted for their humbler manners and moderate lifestyles. They worry about their facial features, outfits, what they say, how they react to other people, and much more. They are very insecure about their self-image, and when you expect them to do chores, study more, or dress more appropriately, you make them feel like they're dangerously close to the "loser" territory.

Your child's self-esteem is under vicious attack every day, even in the best circumstances. So, when an issue arises in which you anticipate stress, first try to take a few minutes to breathe, pray, and diffuse anger that could otherwise lead to thoughtless outbursts and hurtful words. Every time you do this, you teach and model your child to do the same. Then ask your child if they know what the consequences of the mistake are and if they have any ideas on the solution for a better outcome next time. Let them know you value their well-being and mind and trust them to work on their decision-making process. This practice is an excellent opportunity to give your child undivided attention and seek out how your child is feeling and thinking. They might appreciate that you love them enough to kindly want to be available to hear about what is troubling their heart and mind or their concerns of not fitting in, feeling stressed, or another struggle. Almost every time, your child secretly craves your attention, acknowledgment, approval, and help to manage difficult situations. This de-escalation process brings the anger down on the mood elevator and deepens your bond with your child because they feel your grace and love in the same way we feel from our heavenly Father.

You are growing alongside your teen, so don't be afraid to humble yourself when you genuinely feel they have a point. After all, your other relationships are a two-way street. You wouldn't expect anyone else to follow your wishes, so why have such expectations for your child? A scripture in Psalms says, "Search me, God, and know my heart; put me to the test and know my anxious thoughts and see if there is any hurtful way in me and lead me in the everlasting way." (New American Standard Version Bible, 2020, Ps. 139: 23-24) Don't be afraid to admit that you made a mistake if you have made one. No teenager ever lost respect for a humble parent or teacher. The truth is the exact opposite: Teenagers don't respect those people who appear fake to them. Fixing your relationship with the child requires looking deep inside and acknowledging your wrongdoings, repenting for them before your child and God. Let your child know that you don't consider yourself a perfect person and admit to making mistakes when you do. Also, let your child know that when you're setting limitations, it's not because you think little of them but because you want to protect them from repeating and living with mistakes that may have devastating consequences such as suffering from the effects of drugs or living with an incurable sexually transmitted disease.

Evaluate what you can and can't realistically expect from your child. You might be dreaming of a perfect family with well-behaved children who are accepted and achieve at school and obey at home without protest. It's impossible to find such a family. Consider whether your current expectations are realistic and how to change them to be more manageable. Also, make sure you always come from a place of love and understanding when evaluating your child's behavior. Ask yourself if their age and development allow them to meet your expectations and set the bar somewhat higher than their current abilities but not too high so they can't reach them. Understanding your child and where their limitations lie, including those situations and tasks where they could benefit from extra help, is essential to set an expectation the child will want to reach.

All children are terrified of losing parental love. They may not be showing it, but your child loves you more than they love anyone else in this world. Yet they might block that feeling if they don't feel like you love and accept them in return. It is possible for a child to feel this, especially if most home interactions revolve around fulfilling duties rather than loving and caring for one another. Remember, your teen wants to be useful and prove themselves to you but might not be doing that if they fear failure or criticism. Perhaps they fear that it will never be enough, no matter how hard they try. Instead of finding something to criticize, nurture a "good enough" climate in your home. Be happy that their room is "clean enough," that they've studied enough to complete their assignments, and that they are putting in enough effort to fulfill their potential. Make that "enough" the only standard for loving your child as they are and for who they are. Remember that God is strong in our weaknesses, so God will also meet them in their weaknesses.

For example, when you feel like the child should work more on their tidiness, you can praise their effort to keep their room orderly and still guide them to do better. Let me give you an example of when a son cleaned his room. The room was immaculate. Yet when mom opened the closet door, it was messy because he threw almost everything in there, so she said, "Great job on cleaning your room! Now let's work on the closet. Let's throw out the pizza box and set up a time when we can take the rest of all this stuff out and sort out what you want to donate. You can decide what you want to throw away and what you want to keep and organize."

Unconditional love is God's love for us, but we find it so hard to love Him back the same way. Some people block their love for God overall when going through hardship. They think God doesn't love them because some things happened or didn't happen.

If you don't want your child to feel this way about you, then first exercise unconditional love for God and then unconditional love for your family. Unconditional means, for better or worse, sickness and health without expectations.

Many parents feel denying love when the child misbehaves is a good idea, but it's the exact opposite. Refusing love can make your child feel like you never truly loved them and that you'll only love them if they meet your expectations. This concept is a dangerous territory where the child can generalize the notion of only loving when things are good and then denying love in the face of challenges. You might taste your own medicine in that regard, and your child can have difficulty forming long-term, meaningful connections. To love as Jesus did is to love people even when they disappoint or wrong you. Ideally, your unconditional love for God should reflect how you treat your family, so strive to do so as much as possible. Spending as much time with them as possible will give you insight into how they want to be loved, whether through words of encouragement, lots of hugs, or simply time.

Tumultuous teen-parent relationships are nothing new. If you're less than happy with the relationship with your child, you're not alone. It's painful to hear your child say harsh things to you and to see them avoid talking to you at all costs. Never lose hope! Remember, your child loves you. Now that you're on a mission to repair the relationship with your child, you're probably wondering what the first steps are. Well, the first step is to evaluate the past several years of your life and figure out when the relationship went downhill. Perhaps your child's expectations were not met, causing you to grow apart. Either mistakes were made, or difficult circumstances prevented you from being present in the past. The longer you think about it, the more it appears you'll never be able to have a close relationship with your teen again. Please don't believe it! The enemy is planting those seeds of doubt to keep you alienated from your child, but if you're reading this book, it means you genuinely want to repair your broken relationship with your child, and with your faith, God will do it. There are things that you can do to reconnect with your child and build up on the foundations of your previous relationship.

Too often, we're unsure about whether we're doing things right. We doubt our own decisions and choices, yet we are to do the best for our family. We need to believe we're right, or we'd constantly fear making mistakes. But what happens when our sense of self-righteousness hurts the child? You know that you're not supposed to lash out at them. You discipline them severely so they never skip class again, simply because you're petrified about what could happen to them as they roam the town on their own. You hope that spending extra time together will compensate for it, but it doesn't. Your teen is further retreating into their shell, and you can feel that they are shutting you out. Someone must take the first step, and that person is yourself. You might find it challenging but approaching your child and apologizing for anything you've done wrong helps them open their heart to you. It allows them to see you as an honest, caring person rather than an old-fashioned oppressor who doesn't want them to be happy.

Most children feel this way when parents get angry at them, regardless of whether they've done something to cause the outburst. When apologizing, never give explanations or excuses or blame the teenagers or other people for the conflict. It is counter-effective because it may come across as justifying the actions rather than genuinely apologizing.

Even if they disobey or make a wrong decision, and though they might still shut you out, rest assured that the doors have opened at least by an inch. They will, almost certainly, come around and acknowledge their error. It's worth it! Keep working at it.

Most teenagers see asking for forgiveness as something humiliating, but you know better than them that it is not. It's a demonstration of maturity. The second step in earning your child's forgiveness is following through to avoid repeating mistakes. Make sure to respect the child's feelings when conversing without demanding that they reciprocate the same apologetic approach. This interaction shouldn't feel forced. Teenagers should also apologize for their wrongdoings once they genuinely mean it. They should be allowed time to reflect on their actions, and once they come to terms and are ready to take responsibility for their part in the conflict, their apology will be true and honest.

When mending broken relationships, avoid harshness in your voice or posture when approaching your teen. Allow yourself to be vulnerable, genuine, and emotional. When one or both are not completely honest, it hinders the relationship. If your child decides to make themselves vulnerable and share their thoughts, hear them out. Don't interrupt them or dismiss their feelings. They are a child, after all, and they will have exaggerated feelings about events and situations that you wouldn't find stressful at all. However, there is a better time to school your child about emotional regulation and self-control; after all, teens usually do have mood swings. Now's the time to be quiet, listen, let them vent, and hug them if they want. Be firm in stating that you won't tolerate disrespect. If they disrespect you with their words or rolling eyes, tell them you will be ready to listen and be there for them when they are ready to have a conversation with respect. Then walk away. They will probably take some time and think about how they were acting or overreacting while you were so calm and collected. Although there may be issues that you still can't figure out or compromise on, it's essential to show an understanding of how the child feels and reassure them that with prayer and time, God will show you a way to resolve them.

Perhaps the child is ready to move on, or perhaps they haven't forgiven you just yet. Give them time and show patience. After all, the main purpose of an apology isn't to get the child to say what you want them to say but to take accountability for your actions and let them know you're sorry. Maybe they're not yet ready to forgive. Give them some space and let them process their emotional roller coaster before moving on. If things still haven't been resolved between you, then there's something else that you didn't previously consider. Continue to pray for God to convict them and move on their heart so they might be receptive. They might be ready to talk some more. Also, pray for God's wisdom and the right words to say. Pray for God's conviction in their heart. With faith and time, they will come around and apologize to you for their wrongdoing also.

Going back to Paula's situation, she spent a full week during Christmas break with Matthew by taking him on a road trip. It was just her and her son. She explained the situation to her boyfriend that she would see him after Christmas and he was understanding. After more time of pouring into her relationship with her son and some prayers, Matthew warmed up to her boyfriend. Primarily, you want to commit to a growing relationship with God so then you can begin to better nurture your relationship with your teen with respect, humility, and love. Once the seeds of love are sown, don't let the plant wither or die. The next chapter explains how this can happen.

2

THE REAL ADVERSARY

Simply hearing the word "faith" can evoke different feelings depending on your past experiences. Some parents may feel unworthy or too far gone to have faith. Perhaps you've felt let down by God and, despite your best efforts, couldn't find it in your heart to move past injustices. You might have felt disappointed that the help you were praying for didn't arrive while so many other people got away with terrible acts. Now ask yourself, could your anger and disappointment have been misplaced? Have you been blaming God for your misfortune or the true culprit, people, and groups who are directly responsible for the painful experiences you had?

Let me tell you a story to illustrate what anger displacement does. One day, a mother was sitting at home with her daughter, making lunch. A girl heard a knock on the door and ran to open it before her mother could react. Unfortunately, intruders barged in, intending to rob the family. The mother became frantic and attempted to shout for help, which prompted one intruder to shoot her. Now being a witness to a murder, the girl was about to be shot herself. The tragedy ended when the girl's father shot at the intruders from the top of the staircase, causing them to run away. While the little girl and her father survived, they lost a mother and a wife.

You can imagine what a child in mourning would feel in these circumstances. The traumatized girl was seemingly doing better, and after some time in recovery, she returned to school. Yet her father didn't know that she felt furious that her mother had died. Initially, her anger was toward the mother's actual killers, who authorities pursued. Beyond anyone's sight, the intruders saw a solution to their worries by eliminating the only witness to the murder they committed.

One day, they approached the girl through the fence at the school playground. It didn't take long to deceive the girl as they told her she should come with them, saying her father had betrayed her. He had failed to show up on time as soon as her mother cried for help. He was too slow to load a gun; perhaps he was too busy resting to save the girl and her mother in time. From the little girl's perspective, the disappointment in her father's lack of protection became even more significant than the pain she felt from the loss her mother and the anger she felt toward the intruders. The dark offer came: the girl should choose another family, and she would never be hurt or disappointed again.

The girl's father never saw his daughter again. She had gone missing, and no investigation or search party ever recovered her. On the other side of the country, a gang lured her in. Even though these men killed her mother and then abducted and abused her, the girl's anger toward her father grew. She was terrorized and traumatized. The kidnappers constantly reminded her that her father had allowed her to lose her mother and get kidnapped.

Meanwhile, the father never gave up on his child. Years and decades went by, but his love for his daughter never withered. His door remained open for her to return, and he continued the rest of his life looking for her.

If there's anything you can learn from this story, it's that anger can be misplaced. The true adversary isn't the Father but the enemy working through the harmful influences on your teen and perhaps even on you.

As of August 2022, the NIH has reported studies that parents overall have suffered mental health decline due to recent global events involving illness, loss of life, and economic and financial strain. Sadly, this anxiety and depression will spill over to others, including their children. Many parents may feel God punishes them for their minor sins yet allows many others to live unscathed. It is a common thought for many at one point or another, but it's a seed of doubt planted in your mind by the enemy. Yes, the devil is the enemy. Indeed, many challenges make you feel like you've suffered unjustly while others thrive, undeserving of their privilege. You might even blame God for not preventing your bad experiences, not protecting you, and not helping when you needed help. Now, ask yourself, who is the true culprit for your misfortune? Is it God?

This notion may be unsettling to ponder but be patient and give yourself time. Reflect on the possibility that you unintentionally might be on the enemy's side when falling victim to these thoughts. Are there beliefs you hold and things you do purely out of anger? Maybe your cause is essential and relevant, but your motivations affect your actions much more than you know. To protect your child from negative influences, start with those you're not noticing that you haven't thought of questioning yourself. Are there any coming from you? If anger toward God drives you to harmful behaviors, those behaviors also steal your joy, harm your family, and distance your children from you. You could be provoking your child, causing your child to be angry at you. The "blame game" can last for years, destroying your quality of life and the precious time you could spend with your family.

Perhaps the first step could be revealing what makes you blame God. Is it an event in your past that inflicted pain? Poverty? Injustice? Think about things that frustrate you the most and identify who the true enemy is in your situation. Rather than turning to the enemy to fuel your anger, turn to God and His love. If you still feel it's hard to get past specific painful experiences, think about the following.

Remember that Scripture teaches us about a loving, forgiving God who never leaves your side. If the pain keeps you from healing, remember what it felt like trying to feed your hungry baby. Your toddler was, at least once, hungry, screaming for food. Yet when you wanted to feed them, they would push the spoon away, spilling the meal on the floor in frustration. Can you be sure that a solution was available in times of your worst frustration, but you couldn't see it? Sometimes we get so sad and angry that we fail to feel and see God's love and the help He sends us. God isn't numb. He hurts when you hurt. Remember, He also felt pain when He came to earth as a man, but He suffered more than we will ever experience. To heal, you need to be able to abandon anger and sadness and give your burden to God. Romans chapter 5 reassures of this as it says, "And not only this, but we also celebrate in our tribulations knowing that tribulation brings about perseverance; and perseverance, proven character, and proven character, hope; and hope does not disappoint, because the love of God has been poured out within our hearts through the Holy Spirit who was given to us." (New American Standard Version Bible, 2020, Rom. 5:3-5)

Strangely enough, people tend to want to resist healing, fearing to let off anger and accept divine compassion. This tendency is also recorded in psychology as a tendency to avoid forgiveness and recovery at the expense of clinging to pain and anger. In a way, people are like this to maintain a sense of control. As long as we're angry, we're not feeling powerless, and we keep that deeply demeaning feeling on a short leash. To give up anger and frustration often means giving up our ambitions, goals, and inaccurate beliefs associated with the experience. God wants to heal you because you are His child. Seek Him and ask Him. He is waiting for you to embrace His love and healing. Accept the healing He has provided as it says in 1 Peter 2:24 that by his wounds you were healed. Let go of your doubts and trust God's promises. By releasing this anger, you allow God to work on you and through you so that you can reach your child's heart.

As a parent, you will face challenges when raising a teen. What morals and values should you teach so that your child meets the world as it is with a clear direction? Raising younger children is more straightforward in that regard. When in doubt, they'll ask you a question and accept your response as accurate. That way, they begin to form their own belief and value system. It might appear as if you're on the right track. Your young child can discern right from wrong, albeit with your frequent guidance. They show compassion and are willing to acknowledge a mistake when in the wrong. What happens when they reach their teen years? So many questions arise that you need more time to answer for yourself.

Admittedly, your presence and guidance are essential. If you don't answer your child's dilemma, someone else will. That other person, be it a classmate or a group (online or offline), may not have your child's best interest at heart. Maybe they have good intentions and are deeply persuaded by the righteousness and accuracy of their answer. Yet the "outside" guidance too frequently comes from another vision that an individual or a group wishes to fulfill. That vision, or an intention that we sometimes call "agenda," can create confusion or friction between you and the teen. Not everyone intends to harm a child directly or teach them something harmful. Yet the harm often comes in how a message echoes in a young mind that's still impressionable, eager to accommodate and be accepted but still not fully formed and able to think critically.

Discerning what you'll present as good or evil to your child is a moral problem. Teach them that something is universally good, and you risk a teen accepting and condoning all behaviors and attitudes that come with the territory without sufficient critical thinking. Label something entirely evil, and you risk your child developing fears, intolerance, harsh judgment, and even adversity toward other people, which can become destructive.

At this point, parents need standards and boundaries to live and teach. God gave humanity the Ten Commandments through Moses.

God's standards, the moral law, clearly show that He is Holy and we are not. Because humans are sinful by nature, it's impossible to consistently live by them and not break one or more of them at some point. Everyone has either lied, stolen, or coveted something or someone. Thank God that because Jesus died on the cross, we are no longer under this law. God sent us his son Jesus, and it is through His death that the penalty for all our sins is paid. By grace, we are saved. Of course, we can't continue sinning and breaking the commandments. We should repent of sin and strive to be blameless before God so we can live in closeness with Him. When we do the right thing and are at peace with our Savior, we live our best life as He intends. Because we trust in Jesus, He helps us overcome the power of sin and spiritual death. We can also live a better physical life on earth and a promised spiritual eternal life. This path is what God wants for us. He doesn't force it on us, but offers it to us so that we may humbly come to Him seeking this gift.

We want this life of obedience to God for our teens, but we want them to strive for this for themselves. Trying to make them live a certain way forcefully and harshly may push them away from God and us. But if we invest time and love into our teens, the seeds we plant onto their path will most likely take root and blossom into fruitful lives. Without setting the standards and boundaries based on commandments in God's Word, your teen is by far more likely to go with the flow and become agnostic by adopting the conventional norms that outsiders create, which is generally the narrative of doing and believing "whatever feels right to you for the moment." Whenever our teens or we make mistakes, we must go back to the Bible for direction. We must repent and trust in Jesus for His mercy. Ultimately every individual must decide to choose to serve themselves or God.

God's perfect parenting is evident in His relationship with us. If you think about it, God shelters us from thousands of unpredictable circumstances. However, we may suffer consequences when we step out of the boundaries God has placed for us. Without God's protection, we are exposed to dangers of which we're unaware. People make mistakes daily, yet God still forgives and provides love and comfort. Many of the problems adults carry throughout their lives, particularly in their families, come from troubled relationships with fathers. Distant, cold, or abusive fathers leave a mark on adult men and women. Those who haven't had a close relationship with their parents might also struggle to establish healthy relationships with their spouses and children. Troubled relationships with parents cause adults to develop dysfunctional behaviors and habits like addiction.

Yet if your relationship with your parents hasn't been close, there's not much you can do about it as an adult. You may try to improve the relationship to the best possible degree, but most people never quite manage to address the hurt and childhood trauma with their parents in ways that would provide closure. You still have a Father who always looks down on you, keeping His arms open whenever you're ready to ask for help and healing.

Ah, but who would ask for help when we're so keen on figuring things out on our own? You must have observed your child struggle—whether, with school, friendships, or any other kind of a problem—and yet the last thing they'll do is turn to you for help and guidance. Now you're watching them struggle and stress out, patiently waiting for them to come to you since you know that offering help or "meddling" would annoy them. Can you help your child if they're not asking for help? Hardly. You're there, waiting to step in at any moment, yet your child keeps shying away from you, not even wanting to admit they have a problem. They won't admit it to themselves to avoid facing the reality of either making a mistake or owning up to some of their flaws. So, they keep on struggling to get themselves out of an awkward situation, and you, ready and willing to step in, are being shunned and ignored. Now ask yourself: Is it possible that you've been doing the same in your relationship with God? People deal with problems in two ways: either by calming down and thinking through a situation, asking for support, and talking to their close ones about the best ways to move forward, or by keeping troubles to themselves, screaming, being angry, and conniving, and trying to get themselves out of a bad situation by any means while desperately wanting to look like everything is alright.

Now, ask yourself whose help you elicit with these two different responses. Do you turn to God for protection, wisdom, and strength? Or do you run around in a frenzy doing what you'll later deem the worst possible thing? Turning to God when in trouble means letting go of the need to appear well and proud at all costs and humbling yourself before Him and those people who you trust. Talk to your child's teacher and admit that you don't know how to handle a situation or speak with your trusted friends and let them know you're struggling to maintain peace within your family. You can experience healing if you go to people who love you and before God. Turning your back on God when in trouble is almost a habit that we do spontaneously, as children hide from their parents to avoid embarrassment. To prevent this, reaffirm your relationship with God as a parent first and foremost. Do so by reflecting on the following points.

God is unconditionally patient and loving. He's always available to hear your prayers.

God loves you unconditionally. You don't have to work to earn His love. God sent his only son Jesus to die for you and pay your sin debt. There's nothing you can do for God to stop loving you just as you are.

God always does what's best for you. He always has your best interest at heart, even when He disciplines you—the same way you love and protect your child.

God has perfect timing. God knows your future and sees the bigger picture. If something you hoped to do, achieve, or experience isn't yet happening, God thinks it's too early for you.

God already knows everything. The Holy Spirit is with those who follow Him. There's no reason to try hiding anything from your Father because He already knows it. You can feel comfortable bringing your deepest struggles and being honest with yourself and the Lord.

Do you ever notice you repeat a cliche or phrase that your parents used to tell you? A common one is, "If your friends decide to go and jump off a cliff, are you also going to go and jump off the cliff?" Of course, your teen rolls their eyes, but sadly many teens, and adults, tend to follow the crowd. It's very easy when celebrities make clever statements like "I'm living my truth" or "I have my truth, and you have yours." These influential people are an instrument for the real adversary who seeks to deceive and confuse. But this is a cop-out for doing what's right. It's their free pass to do or say what they want without criticism or correction. A parent who wants to be effective in raising a teen must establish what truth is. Should the definition of truth flex to fit one's lifestyle preference at that moment and then be adjusted when circumstances change? Then it wouldn't be truth, would it? It would be scary for teens to believe they have their own truth. What you want to do is establish THE truth. Jesus said, "I am the way, the truth, and the life. No one comes to the Father except through me (New American Standard Version Bible, 2020, John 14:6). Jesus' truth is the absolute truth and should be the framework for implementing standards for yourself as a parent and your teen.

The Bible isn't only a piece of literary legacy. It is a chronicle of early Christian and Jewish life, aside from being a foundation of Christian teaching. It came directly from God and was written under His inspiration. You can encourage your teen to read the Bible, contemplate, and ask questions when confused or in doubt about anything. Dr. Jason Lisle, a Christian astrophysicist, states that even atheist scientists unwittingly depend on a biblical worldview to account for things necessary for scientific testing logically. The Bible is a lifeline, a compass to return to when facing struggles or temptations. If you and your teen find the Bible mysterious or difficult to understand, use a version like New American Standard Bible and Bible study aids or devotional apps like Our Daily Bread app or YouVersion mobile app. Always validate Bible studies and books by checking them against Bible Scriptures. Pray for God to help you and your child discern what is true and acceptable. The following passage is found in Proverbs:

My son, do not forget my teaching, but keep my commands in your heart, for they will prolong your life many years and bring you peace and prosperity. Let love and faithfulness never leave you; bind them around your neck and write them on the tablet of your heart. Then you will win favor and a good name in the sight of God and man. (New American Standard Version Bible, 2020, Proverbs 3:1–4)

Why does God warn His people not to forget His teaching? Parents must be mindful that just as there is truth, there are lies. There are so many talking heads constantly demanding our attention and our children's attention. John 8:44 is the Scripture that says the devil is the father of all lies, the author of confusion, using any means to confuse minds, whether through media, celebrities, or education. The following chapters expose the subtle but cunning ways he does this.

Step two in fostering the closer parent-teen relationship is knowing who the real adversary is, the deceiving devil, but also knowing God is more powerful and we can turn to Him to guide us and trust Him to help us guide our children to overcome the enemy. You may wonder how exactly the adversary targets our teens and what we can do about it. Let's start with the most common way the enemy intrudes into our lives.

3

INTRUSIVE TECHNOLOGY

A National Center for Biotechnology Information (NCBI) meta-analysis in August of 2022 showed that environmental stressors, including social isolation due to home confinement, lack of physical exercise, and fear of catching a virus, significantly increased anxiety and depression in children. There is also no doubt these stressors are a factor in pushing children deeper into their electronic devices. Most would agree that many corporations and organizations had more to gain than children during this crisis. The biggest issue with organizations like these is that they don't operate to benefit your child's growth and development. They're advocating for their own goal or cause and often don't pay sufficient attention to how their representatives' words and actions affect children. Not all these organizations are inherently good or bad. Some we can hardly argue with, like movements advocating for a healthier lifestyle or keeping kids away from drugs. Others are morally gray and revolve around a perceived injustice that children should know about to be more mindful of their daily lives. These causes revolve around social inequalities, injustices, and often tragic events that point out a need for societal change. What makes them morally gray are two essential aspects:

- the lack of justification for involving children. Many social media groups and communities target teenagers as potential contributors to their cause. Still, they lack argumentation regarding why it is necessary and justified to include children in their work. These socially oriented groups often concern themselves with matters beyond children's understanding. When they simplify their messages to a certain degree, these messages become superficial and inaccurate. No social problem can be reduced to a slogan or a narrative suitable for teenagers—at least, not successfully—without causing a degree of elusiveness. After all, if teenagers could understand and resolve social inequalities, why have institutions and facilities? Why not leave it up to teenagers to write laws and build the world according to their vision?

- the lack of transparency regarding how the organizations operate and what justifies their actions and activities. You've likely heard more than once that an organization was involved in criminal activities, like theft, given that the prominent figures who led the organization frequently withheld donation funds for themselves, leaving those in need of assistance empty-handed. Everyone involved with the organization, including teenagers who'd put a lot of work into fundraisers, would feel heartbroken and doubtful of the idea of doing charity overall.

It is a parent's prerogative to do background checks and research communities and organizations with which your child is involved. You have the right and reasoning to assert boundaries regarding your child's involvement with other groups and organizations. You can talk with your child about why these organizations don't offer a solution; the root of the problem is that we live in a broken world with sinful human nature. But what happens when these groups and organizations are obscure? When neither parents nor teachers know that they exist, these groups are exposing them to atrocious images of violence and abuse, attempts at manipulation, and even coercion to violence.

In this chapter, you'll learn how destructive these obscure communities can become. You'll learn about the evil lurking from within your child's screen, often disguised as a friendly avatar or a game character. You'll also learn how to track your child's online activities, intervene when needed, and teach your child to use social media responsibly.

Have you ever wondered why Steve Jobs and Bill Gates's children didn't get their gadgets until they turned 14? Even then, their online activities were monitored and controlled. Both billionaires emphasized time spent with the family and mealtimes completely free of electronics. Rather than spoiling their kids and teaching them internet addictions, these two moguls focused their parenting efforts on education, culture, history, and the more scientific side of technology. After all, the role of technology is to make people's lives easier, so their children get the kind of intelligent upbringing that teaches them to use technology for personal growth. Yet not all parents have the same relationship with their children. Often, we're busy and tired from work, and we want to keep kids quiet and out of the way. Other times, we don't want to ruffle feathers or want to get along with our children. Our minds revert to how we felt being teenagers when our parents called everything we liked harmful, unhealthy, and destructive. Often, parents need to learn how fast technology is developing so they can monitor their children.

In front of your very eyes, your child might be falling into internet addiction. They might be using questionable apps seemingly designed for personal growth. When facilitated by experts, motivational speeches, meditations, and breathing exercises are valid forms of self-development for well-informed adults. Yet the current internet policies allow anyone to become a mentor overnight. They need start-up money, charisma, and skill to do online research. Before you know it, influencers are born with social media facilitating their access to teens. But why is this such a big problem?

Influencers can be very strategic in captivating your child's attention to convey twisted and unsubstantiated ideas, which is very dangerous. At the very least, we can view the whole New Age spirituality movement as quite unhealthy. It distances teenagers from faith in God by instilling a sense of insecurity. Thinking "outside the box" relativizes everything teenagers need clearly defined, from right and wrong to healthy and unhealthy. While mature adults can successfully navigate these influences and disregard what they perceive as harmful, teenagers don't possess such an advanced level of critical thinking. They need a transparent value system and a sense of morality to feel safe. The closest they come to that is by internalizing Biblical values taught within their family. When these values sometimes clash with what modern society imposes, teenagers seek an easier value system that's more flexible. This kind of moral flexibility can quickly lead to anxiety and depression. Initially, teenagers get "hooked" on instant dopamine boosts provided by inspiring images, speeches, messages, and podcasts. Most of these contents advocate a line of thinking too idealistic to pass the real-world test. The more teenagers engage with online influencers and "mentors," the more they become emotionally sensitive.

For example, as a parent, you would teach your teenager honesty. Yet honesty is a two-edged sword, so your teen might have a problem with being expected to be honest while everyone else seems to lie whenever it pleases them. Their online motivational speakers then teach them a different lesson: to keep their thoughts and visions to themselves and turn their back on "haters." Your teen is then consumed in their fantasies, planning for achievements that take far more effort than they can perceive. They retreat into themselves and spend entire afternoons and evenings drowning in motivational content. Yet they're still unable to complete the tasks that lead to achieving what they want (e.g., improving grades, winning competitions, and having more quality friendships). Instead, their online teachings fail the test, and they return to consuming more harmful online content because they believe the fault lies with them. If they think they failed at applying the said spiritual and motivational strategies correctly, their perspective of the world and their self-image become skewed as their self-esteem diminishes.

However, faith and confidence in God's word teach us to grow and advance in a more genuine, realistic fashion. The Bible says in Joshua, "This Book of the Law shall not depart from your mouth, but you shalt meditate on it day and night, so that you may be careful to do according to all that is written in it; for then you will make your way prosperous, and then you will achieve success. (New American Standard Version Bible, 2020, Josh. 1:8)

Acting with integrity and doing the right thing is no longer popular. Your children need to accept that some people will like them, and others won't, and that's okay. Help them learn to take the time to study, analyze all sides of arguments that challenge their faith against Biblical standards, and become critical thinkers.

Most parents know that harmful content comes mostly through social media and games, but do they know to what extent?

Teenagers are highly impressionable. They're always afraid of missing out on trends and doing dangerous things just to fit in. Your kid might seem different, and perhaps they are. But you can never be too certain that a crush or a best friend won't influence them into doing something harmful. Friends could pressure them into participating in dangerous social trends and challenges that can get them hurt or even get them to hurt someone else.

Social media has become a favorite outlet for teens to keep secrets and live out adventurous fantasies far from their parent's sight. It doesn't help that apps and software develop new functionalities almost every month and making it impossible for parents to keep up. Many parents are unaware that their child could send or receive inappropriate, abusive, or threatening messages via text or social media in the form of hashtags, posts, and challenges. Participating in online trends gives teenagers a sense of belonging. Social media is now a trend that barely any teen is allowed to question. Not having a social media profile is to be invisible and excluded since these platforms facilitate most teens' social activities. If that wasn't bad enough, some individuals and groups are directly out to hurt children.

Now, you must think, who'd want to hurt a child? Spiritually, we can blame the enemy. We can blame evil that is always at work, looking for ways to disfigure and taint everything it can. We can also read about online predators and reflect on what psychologists and psychiatrists claim causes these destructive social media trends. In proven, investigated cases, individuals with severe psychological problems, access to resources, and technological power purposefully create cult-like organizations aimed at teens. These organizations appeal to the teenager's sense of isolation. Some teenagers feel misunderstood and rejected, so they become easy targets. In the beginning, we have vulnerable teenagers on one end and individuals with narcissistic, psychopathic, sociopathic, and sadistic traits on the other. These predators find gratification in dominating, controlling, and hurting teens. This form of abuse is safer for the abuser, though, as the teenager is the one who commits any crime. In the case of dangerous online challenges, online predators relish their infamy and the attention they get. Any talk of the harmful nature of the trend amuses them. It empowers their sense of notoriety, which is partially why questionable online personalities are hard to sanction.

Now persons like these sometimes operate on their own, and other times they form a team. They design challenges on platforms like TikTok, Instagram, and Facebook. The goal is that a teen will repeat the challenge and post about it, from which a predator gets the gratification of getting kids to do what they want. Sadly, they get even more gratification if teenagers go too far and injure themselves or someone else.

Dangerous traps that teenagers might fall prey to on social media include:

- sending provocative and explicit images far from parents' sight.

- creating false social media profiles to "catfish" other people close to them. To "catfish" means contacting other people while pretending to be a different person.

- going into a trance and inducing states of altered consciousness. Spiritually, this is associated with summoning evil forces while psychologically having the same harmful effect as hallucinogens and psychedelic drugs. A disturbing TikTok trend known as "Red Door Yellow Door" has been known to put participants in a state of trance, after which they experience mental problems.

- self-harm and harm to others (e.g., the "blackout" challenge, which resulted in several children's deaths). This challenge instructed teens in numerous ways of choking themselves.

Advise your child to think carefully before sending texts and photos via message because their messages stay online forever and might have harmful consequences, sometimes years later. Advise the child against sending any message they wouldn't feel comfortable showing to their grandparents.

Every school provides internet access to students, and it's only sometimes filtered or monitored. Parents can be sure to review the school's internet safety policies and get involved in school board meetings to raise concerns. Sadly, children as young as 11 are exposed to pornography on a school device. The risks for psychological harm will always be out there, but if teens have internalized their Biblical values, they will feel secure about guarding their hearts and minds. They're more likely to share with their parents what they saw, heard, or experienced at school if they feel secure that their parents won't react irrationally but instead love them no matter what.

Ask your teen if they know how to monitor the amount time they spend on their favorite apps. If they don't know, figure out together how much time is spent in a day, a week, and even a month, and ask your teen if they are comfortable spending that amount of time on those apps. Ask them to think of what else they could have accomplished during this time: something creative, getting ahead on schoolwork or earning extra money, etc.

If your teen wants help reducing phone or screen time, offer them tips such as putting the phone away in another room an hour before bed, not bringing the phone to the table at mealtime, and turning off notifications from all apps to be less distracted. If your teen wants to excel and be more productive and less dependent on a device, help them view phones and devices as tools for creativity and purpose, not just entertainment. In other words, be more intentional about using the phone for setting up a time to meet up with friends in person, to be organized and manage time using the calendar to schedule tasks for the day, to find locations using maps, to build a website or search for a summer job. Having plans and not letting social media be a distraction will result in success. Share the Scripture, "Let's not become discouraged in doing good, for in due time we will reap if we do not become weary." (New American Standard Version Bible, 2020, Gal. 6:9)

Gaming isn't all fun and games. Addiction is a well-researched phenomenon that predates the internet and social media addictions. Video games, which are technically "older" than the internet, have long been known to be addictive. In the modern era, it's never been easier for teenagers to develop an addiction to gaming. We may say that the current social climate provides little, if any, sense of safety to teenagers. A lifestyle confined by rules leaves little space for adventure, so teens turn to games in pursuit of challenge and adrenaline. Gaming, sadly, can create the same addiction as illegal drugs and alcohol. It can alter teenagers' consciousness so severely that they neglect their biological needs. Excessive gaming compromises their friendships and school performance. Some games are openly destructive, which we can see in the example of the game called *Cult of the Lamb*. In this game, the leading player becomes possessed by an "empowering" force. They are supposed to build their community, gain followers, and create a cult. However, they must apply aggressive strategies of indoctrinating digital "opponents" using either persuasion or violence. Luckily, most teenagers would find this game off-putting. However, teenagers struggling with anger, depression, addiction, and more severe mental problems might feel inclined to enjoy this game and take their fantasies into real life.

How does one battle such destructive influences? First, let's correctly identify what is truly an adversary. The above example was easy but there are instances of highly manipulative games, cartoons, and TV shows that use the same pattern but in a finer cloak. It's much harder to discern the enemy's intentions in games with aesthetics and symbols that glorify darkness but are not as obvious. The answer to knowing your adversary lies in God's Word: "Be sober-minded; be watchful. Your adversary, the devil, prowls around like a roaring lion seeking someone to devour" (New American Standard Version Bible, 2001, 1 Peter 5:8).

Parents can look out for these inappropriate games and other dangers we will discuss further here. Teens associate their self-worth with their game characters and avatars. Cyberbullying predators are aware of this and easily bully these vulnerable gamers, affecting their mental health. Many of these cyber-bullies your teens could be playing with online are adults disguising themselves as teens to earn trust initially. They'll end up being verbally abusive, manipulative, and sexually abusive. They can also hack into internal cameras and microphones. Parents can refer to guidelines with their children to be informed and protect themselves. A parent should immediately report any predators' abuse on the gaming platforms to law enforcement.

When it comes to gaming, it's vital to separate gaming addiction from the occurrence of violence associated with gaming. When we observe the link between gaming and violence, we go on to the assumption that violent games cause violent behavior. This assumption has been disproven by many studies, but there is a link to circumstances in which violence occurs. It is accurate that a violent game itself is less likely to cause real-life violence than most people presume. However, gaming can be, and in many cases, has been, a significant contributor to worsening mental health conditions that lead to accidents and violence. In a way, gaming is and isn't to blame for violent incidents in which gamers harm themselves and others. Every teen has emotional issues to a certain degree. They have insecurities, a desire to fit in, a lack of critical thinking, and a sort of group mentality that's quick to accept everything popular in their group. In that sense, teens are journeying from childhood to adolescence and eventually adulthood. At this stage, teenagers have difficulties when it comes to coping with feelings. Every day is a test for their self-esteem, whether it's about school performance or standards within their social circle. Their mental state is forming and either improving, recovering from trauma, or declining into a disorder. The main reason why teenagers so often surprise us with outrageous acts of violence or self-harm is because of how critical that life stage is. The minds of those who are already experiencing mental health issues are at a crossroads, and what we see as a tragic outburst is, in fact, one of the first visible escalations of mental illness. Mood and personality disorders begin to establish themselves in adolescence, and a child exposed to addiction is at risk of dramatic mental health decline. The consequences of this are dire, as you're about to learn.

In 2017, the popular game Pokémon Go led to many deaths from people losing track of their safety while chasing digital Pokémon. Players have not only stepped onto roads without noticing and got hit by vehicles but lost their lives because of trespassing.

In 2018, a mass shooting occurred at a yearly gaming tournament. When a gamer, David Katz (24), lost a series of matches, he engaged in a mass shooting and killed two people while wounding nine at the gaming event.

In 2019, a Ukrainian native, Vasya Turda, stabbed his friend in a gaming quarrel.

Tragedies like these are numerous, albeit rare when we account for the entire population of teens. Yet they remain a reminder to monitor children's gaming habits. Games constantly challenge players and make them exercise focused attention, logic, problem-solving, decision-making, and pattern recognition. If used correctly, gaming can facilitate these and other essential life skills.

If you help your teen choose entertainment wisely, they can grow their creative and cognitive skills. What's important is ensuring that the content presented to your child isn't occultic or inappropriate and that they're not spending an unhealthy amount of time in front of screens. Greg Seaman, the founder of Eartheasy, provides the following tips to keep your child's internet time in check and protect them from the adverse effects of internet and gaming addictions.

#1: Join the Game

Teenagers are hungry for their parent's attention. They might pretend to be more mature than they are and act as if they don't want your company. Don't fall for this! You're the only one who can be their first line of defense when they are gaming. Before you impose rules for what your child can and can't play, first find out what's going on and which games they enjoy. Sit down with them and play some of their favorite games together. Doing this will help you examine each game and decide whether to approve it or give your teen a nudge in a different direction. A conversation with your teen might be, "Let's review this game. Tell me what's good and what's bad about this game. Over time, is it potentially destructive to the mind, heart, and spirit? What are the benefits of playing this game? Do you know the person you are talking to on the other end? Is this a game you would play if your grandma or Jesus sat next to you?" They might laugh at first, but it's a good conversation starter.

#2: Support Their Awareness

We, as parents, might think that "putting your foot down" with a teen is the best approach. This method may not work in your favor, and your insistence that a teen limits their gaming time might encounter much resistance. But what if your child decides to do that on their own? Expose the potential dangers and risks of cyber-bullies and predators to your child. Refer to the Entertainment Software Rating Board (ESRB) to review game ratings together. Teach your child to change their account passwords and keep them secure. It may be a good idea to encourage your child to record how much time they spend gaming for a week. Then you can let them conclude that reducing that time is the best option.

#3: Give Them Options

Remember that teenagers turn to the game in pursuit of challenge and excitement. Once your child sees how much time they're spending online, you can let them know that this time can be better used on other activities, preferably that involve physical activity. For example, they can take up a hobby, sport, or a course that will teach them much more valuable skills.

#4: Give Them Quality Time

Plan how you'll spend time together as a family and help your teen plan their time with friends. Fun, outdoor activities will give your teen the sense of action and excitement they seek.

#5: Help Your Child Set Short- and Long-Term Goals

Goals are a great tool to engage your child and to provide them with focus and motivation to engage in healthy, productive activities. Get your child a planner and ask them to write down short-term and long-term goals they wish to achieve. Then break down those goals into milestones, steps, and tasks your child can complete daily.

#6: Provide Support and Encouragement

We often forget that the things that matter to our children should also matter to us. Parents often dismiss their children's interests due to a lack of time and energy. Not showing interest can make the teen feel rejected and put down. Think more about what your teen likes to do and express support and interest in their healthy activities.

#7: Spend More Time Together as a Family

Always remember that your child wants to spend time with you, even if they're acting like you're uninteresting. This time spent together will strengthen the bond between you and your child, and your teen won't think of you as an obstacle to having a good time. Set aside time for more family activities, including mealtimes and social activities. These activities should occur without screens and electronics and with as much personal and emotional engagement as possible.

Teach your teen to balance their entertainment time with schoolwork and chores, choosing content that honors God's values and standards. Use your parental authority when they don't because allowing them to continue the behavior enables them to continue destructive and possibly sinful habits, which are much more difficult to reverse later. If this approach causes increased conflict, consider counseling for addiction and mental health. But ultimately, they need to prove responsibility and self-control. If you approach your child about these things with love and compassion, you might be surprised at how willing they are to work on changing their own habits. According to a Pew Research Center report, about 60% of teens admit that the amount of time they spend online is a problem. "Like a city that is broken into and without walls, so is a person who has no self-control over his spirit."(New American Standard Version Bible, 2020, Prov. 25:28)

Since this intrusion of the enemy through technology is probably the most common and dangerous area that requires parents' attention, step three of a stronger parent-teen relationship is getting involved and being aware of dangerous messages coming through technology. Creatively find ways to spend more one-on-one time with your teen in other healthy activities and show your teen how to manage tech instead of letting it manage them.

4

INTRUSIVE MEDIA AND CULTURE

Quality entertainment, in appropriate amounts, can be healthy for teenagers. Yet, as we know, the enemy finds a way to corrupt everything. According to the Journal of Adolescent Health, almost half of all music videos involve drugs, including alcohol and tobacco. The Office of National Drug Policy Control states that 71% of TV shows involve the use of alcohol. Based on data such as this, the American Addiction Centers conclude that this type of entertainment does contribute to the increased risk of substance abuse. They also conclude that teens exposed to R-rated movies and social networking sites are at a much higher risk of using marijuana.

Remember, the devil deceived Eve through the serpent. A similar thing is done through culture and media when they pass on seemingly appealing messages that call for barely any critical thinking. For example, when your child hears a message like "You should express how you feel," it is a true statement that can help them if thought through well. If not, a child can easily skew it into justifying harmful or intolerant behavior and even cause self-harm if teenagers feel sad and lonely. The true importance of the content your children watch and listen to comes from the messaging. Content can include melodies, plots, and characters that look appealing and relatable to teenagers. Characters can be of their age and dress and talk similarly. They can even have the same insecurities and face the same challenges. Yet the main "point" of each program lies in the message and philosophy it advocates. Art schools explicitly teach this concept, educating artists in various spheres to find their philosophy and bring it to life using symbolism. There's nothing wrong with this unless the messages are harmful to children.

It is easy to cloak harmful messages between seemingly age-appropriate lines. The reason is that they're not direct but are instead deductible based on several different messages. For example, if two characters in a TV show engage in crime, and one gets hurt while the other ends up profiting unscathed, the show sends a message that there aren't any consequences for their actions. This outcome isn't actual, of course, but the allure of adventure can sometimes cloud teenagers' judgment to the point where they believe what they want to, not what they know to be true.

Movie and TV entertainment is a cultural phenomenon and a trend that barely any teenager can escape. Yet harmful messages can be found in various films and instill deep insecurities and misconceptions about life and relationships. The synonyms for the word "program" are scheme, plan or plan of action. Interestingly, teenagers who spend a lot of time binging on movies and TV may think that life is easier than it is. Main characters usually have what's sometimes called "plot armor," which means that they never face realistic odds and consequences that a natural person would since they aren't a real person. Characters are supposed to stay in the program until its ending, and they often emerge victorious in situations that many critics find unrealistic. Aside from that, actors and actresses display a look intentionally designed to draw in audiences. They're beautiful, with spotless skin and thin, athletic bodies. Many have an appearance that indicates plastic surgery. Even the most mundane situations are polished for TV, so your child can become overly self-critical. Your teen can't live an upscale lifestyle on minimum wage or have perfectly tidy bedrooms without cleaning. If they try to cause mischief in school, the day won't just go on. The authorities will follow up, and their actions have real consequences.

Perhaps the most harmful influence of the media is on a teen's state of mind and self-image. Some studies show that teenagers are getting more plastic surgeries compared to earlier years. The American Society of Plastic Surgeons performed almost 219,000 plastic surgeries in 2010 on patients between the ages of 13 and 19. Unfortunately, many teens are pressured and influenced into surgeries unnecessarily.

Now's a great time to "peel the onion" and let your child see how false many movies are. Here are some suggestions for how to protect your child against these harmful influences:

- Research the content they watch, read movie reviews with them, and teach them how to do it independently.

- Ask your teen what message the movie sends and how it aligns with their family's values and Biblical standards.

- Talk to your child about the biblical concept of self-worth. Remind them that "We all have equal worth because we're image bearers of God" (New American Standard Version Bible, 2001, Gen. 1:27). We can build our self-esteem, but we can't build or lose our self-worth because it never alters.

- Find alternative movie streaming services that offer family-friendly and even faith-based entertainment.

Again, suppose your teen has internalized the Biblical view of self-worth. In that case, they will be more confident and secure and value themselves despite any mean-spirited, intentional, unintentional verbal attacks against them. They will also naturally feel personal conviction when they see or hear something that contradicts their worldview. In other words, your teen will be a critical consumer, not a passive consumer, and will not readily accept a new idea or theory even if it's repeated multiple times by celebrities. By the way, the term worldview used throughout this book means the foundation on which they perceive the world.

Melody: a rhythmic sound pattern that passes on frequencies and vibrations dear to our hearts. If there was ever a craft with such a significant potential to heal and bring about growth, it's music. While music dates far back into history, science is only now unfolding the God-given mechanisms in which melodies communicate feelings, invoke ideas, and affect thinking. To say music, in general, is somehow harmful or dangerous would be wrong. After all, science demonstrated that classical music, especially instruments made from natural materials, supports infants' and children's development. It's even more curious that the same melody resonates entirely differently in its digital form when played through speakers from a device than when listened to in real-life performances. Music, quite literally, has the potential to make you brighter, healthier, and at peace with the Lord. That is when used wisely.

Such will be the enemy's nature that he will find a way to at least try and corrupt everything good, especially when it comes to the media that attempts to penetrate all defenses. After all, music doesn't ask for our permission to enter our minds and hearts. We respond to it emotionally and unwillingly. Hearing the type of music you don't like can alter your emotional state for the day, just as listening to an uplifting melody can pull you up from the deepest depths of despair.

To say that teenagers should listen to any music they like is the same as saying they should go anywhere they want unmonitored. Left to their own devices, as bright and beautiful as they are, teenagers hardly have any defense against these influences. When you allow a teen to listen to whatever music is popular, you're essentially allowing anyone to seed ideas and feelings into their minds with absolutely no control. Anyone who's ever met a teenager knows you can't select things for them. Teenagers test boundaries as they slowly journey into adulthood and exercise independence. As once your toddler had to fall to learn how to walk and run, these teenagers are now to make mistakes, learn from them, and gain their own experiences to become well-functioning adults. Faith and God's Word in the heart provide an inner compass that helps teenagers discern right from wrong and form self-selected boundaries for their actions which will apply when there's no one around to teach them. Music is a gift from God, especially if it glorifies God and His creation.

Imagine getting up in the morning to find strangers in your home. You ask them who they are, and they tell you they're here to teach your child to rebel against you, test boundaries and beliefs, and experiment with drugs and sexuality. Of course, you'll either grab a phone to call the police or shout at the intruders to leave. Then they begin laughing and tell you there's no way to throw them out. They point to your child sitting by their laptop with headphones on, saying they've been teaching them for years.

God gave us music to worship Him, and through that worship, we grow and experience true happiness: happiness that's not an addictive indulgence but a celebration of life and love. However, much of the mainstream music is different. Some artists do an excellent job at creating music that speaks not only about life but also about the human experience. But what happens when these boundaries shift from human experience to indulging in the celebration of human suffering? When specific musicians present vice and destructive behavior as rebellious and edgy, they do just that—celebrate human suffering. That a young person lives in a crime-ridden neighborhood and harsh environment where they're left to fend for themselves is truly a sad thing, there's nothing fun about it. Yet some artists choose to present various misfortunes as entertaining. Even worse, some forms of music, suitable for adults but often geared to appeal to teenagers, glorify rebellion against society. They blur the lines of value systems from which no child benefits. Anyone well-intentioned wouldn't try to make teenagers feel like the world around them is hopeless, unsafe, and oppressive.

Too often, artists forget just how much children need safety. Child development experts will tell you that it's okay to withhold the truth about a situation from your child if you feel the tragic fact will be detrimental to them. On one occasion, a woman was spared much pain. Her father had committed suicide when she was a young girl, and her mother told her he had died in an accident. The mother only told the rest of the story when the woman finished her psychology studies and could process what was likely going on in her father's mind. Had she learned this truth before she was able to process it, she would have grown up thinking that her father didn't love her and had chosen to leave her. The mother's decision to withhold the whole story, which lasted for over 20 years, contributed to protecting her daughter against hardship that would have been too much for her to handle and would have negatively affected her development.

Yet popular culture is now all about "truth" at all costs, even if it means exposing teenagers to complex issues which will make them question everything they know. Doing so contributes to various mental health issues, so one must wonder what motivation some artists and organizations have to make teenagers feel angry, oppressed, and insecure. You are justified to protect your child from that, even if it means going to great lengths in monitoring what they watch, read, and hear.

Not everything is "black and white" when discussing music. You still need a clear guide to decide whether you're listening to music that's acceptable to God. You can reflect on Philippians 4:8: "whatever is true, whatever is noble, whatever is right, whatever is pure, whatever is lovely, whatever is admirable—if anything is excellent or praiseworthy—think about such things" (New American Standard Version Bible, 2001, Philippians 4:8).

Just as with analyzing games, media, and movies, you can explore the lyrics and story behind a song. A destructive message can be hidden in small details, and you may be able to sense it intuitively but be unable to explain it. Let's take a simple example of a phrase often passed through music: "We should all love each other and get along." This seemingly positive message, without context, may have harmful implications. It doesn't give you that fulfilling, genuine feeling. It's because a part of you is very aware of how a statement like this can be dangerous. To tell a child they should love everyone and always get along could have disastrous consequences, wouldn't it? A child raised in this way would be susceptible and could wander off with anyone who caught their attention. Children need this spiritual discernment with art and entertainment. Messages can be accurate and positive and still result in tragedy if not thought through critically. A simple way to develop your criteria is by looking into the category of messages that the music sends.

The kind of music most suitable for teens will contain either moral or amoral messages. Moral messages promote the teachings of the Bible, although the music doesn't necessarily have to come with a religious note. Today, most ethical systems and reasoning originated from the Bible and thread across science and law. There are also amoral messages, which paint a picture of a theme without relation to biblical teachings. They are more neutral in tone and content and don't advocate for a particular line of thinking. The third category of messages is the one to be wary of, including messages that directly contradict the Bible's teachings. They are called immoral messages, and they glorify ideas that oppose the teachings of the Bible. The key word here is "glorify." It's one thing to observe and note the complexities of moral reasoning, write about its intricacies, and entertain the conundrum that real-life experiences sometimes are regarding the Scripture. However, glorifying something is an entirely different thing. Let's take the example of "We should all love each other and get along." A moral message would be that a person should honor, respect, and feel the highest regard for the people around them to the best of their ability. An amoral message would be that the world becomes constructive when people aim to get along and destructive when they don't and that rules apply to all communities. An immoral message, however, would glorify the idea of profoundly loving a person next to you, no matter who they are, how they treat your or other people, with your whole being. Now, you can see how and in which ways this would go against the Bible's teachings but also against common sense. The issue with the immoral message is that it appeals to adults' and teenagers' weaknesses and insecurities. Immoral messages can persuade teenagers to tap into their hurt, anger, and confusing sensations and intensify them.

Satan is the father of lies and the author of confusion. The occult is considered either creepy, scary, and dangerous by those who disapprove of it or alluring and fun by those who consume it. If you research the most destructive artists out there, you'll reveal that many of them have criminal records, diagnoses of personality disorders, a history of trauma, or all three. If you were ever to listen to their interviews, you'd discover that they perceive the enemy as someone wronged by the Lord; their only desire is to step out of obedience to God and be their own gods in a way because, after all, satanism is about the worship of the self, not Satan, contrary to what most people think. The idea of self-worship is why most secular music lyrics focus on the self. So why is it a surprise that teens are always concerned about themselves if this is what their favorite music tells them?

So, how can you protect your teenager against harmful music and encourage a taste of wholesome music?

First, if your teen has always listened to dark, negative music, don't ban or criticize it. That approach will likely result in anger and rebellion. After all, there is almost no escaping it because they'll hear it at school, friends' houses, games, and so forth. Instead, be as wise as a serpent but gentle as a dove. Ask them questions about their music and movies. Open-ended questions allow them to analyze the content on their own. Play music in the home that honors God. Have a conversation with them about the songs in their playlist and ask the following questions:

Do those songs elevate their mood? Do they know what the lyrics say and the song's overall message? And finally, does that message align with their values? Why do most of the songs glamorize something harmful or destructive? Does it affect your mindset?

Always pray before having these conversations so that God guides you with your tone and non-verbal communication. Try to speak in love with grace to your teen and not come across as critical. Hopefully, the door will open for them to ask why you prefer God-honoring music over rap or hip-hop with derogatory or damaging lyrics. Then you can explain how you strive to live in a way that's pleasing to God, including music choices. You want everything you do to be acceptable to God. There is a Scripture in Psalms that says, "May the words of my mouth and the meditation of my heart be acceptable in Your sight, Lord, my rock and my Redeemer." (New American Standard Version Bible, 2020, Psalms 19:14) The songs you sing or music you listen to affect your mood and either draw your heart toward God or away from Him as your heart meditates on them. To expect an instant change in your child's music preference may be unrealistic, but your child's heart may change as you keep praying, conversing, and playing God-honoring music.

To this end, step four in improving your parent-teen relationship is, again, getting involved by spending time building on conversations around music, movies, books, art, or any form of media and how it impacts culture and your faith-centered worldview.

5

INTRUSION IN EDUCATION

When talking about intruders, let's briefly reflect on the previous chapter and the types of influence we see. As an undeniable factor of influence on children, schools admittedly offer all three types of influence. Moral influences are those that are in line with the Bible's teachings. Most schools strive to teach children to be honest, conscientious people and to help and respect one another. Schools also strive to instill wisdom, intellectual sharpness, and practical abilities needed for a child to succeed. We may call these influences amoral since they don't oppose the Bible's teachings and aren't related to Scripture. However, there are lessons that schools sometimes teach that directly collide with faith values, directly and sometimes subtly. Some of the most challenging topics include the origin of life, LGBTQ issues, racial issues, and gender or sexual identity issues. In this chapter, we'll overview how some aspects of public education undermine faith principles and what you can do to protect your child against influences that collide with your family's beliefs.

Children spend approximately 2210 days at school from kinder through 12th grade, but even for public schools, it's not just science, math, history, language arts, and physical education. It's also religion. Is there such a thing as a non-religious school? In many ways, no. Despite any claims that the curriculum isn't religious in nature, every school has its own educational philosophy. That philosophy determines what teachers believe children need from education, the sort of worldview the school cultivates, the educational policy it advocates for, and the choice of lessons and teaching methods a school uses. According to Doug Wilson, author of *Recovering the Lost Tools of Learning*, it's impossible to separate education and religion because education includes answering questions about religious issues such as the origin of life, morality, the meaning of life, and destiny.

On top of that, each teacher enjoys a great deal of liberty in integrating these philosophies into their teaching style via their worldview. This wouldn't be a problem if there were enough schools to choose from and educational plurality to provide a broad spectrum of options for families who wish to raise children through faith in God. But when there's only a handful of schools in your town, out of which only one or two work for the family in terms of travel and distance, ensuring your child receives an education that honors your family's values becomes a mission. It is your mission, one of the most important since it is a significant part of shaping your child's mind, discipline habits, and worldview for a lifetime.

This mission isn't easy, especially if you have been unaware of the full scope of moral and philosophical lessons taught to children. You may be able to look at your child's curriculum and school policies but still, need to catch on to the fine print of what schools have or don't have the right to do. An important job as a parent is to be wary of influences that make an impression on your child and know that you're fully entitled to make educational choices for them while they're underage.

In this chapter, we'll address how you can navigate educational influences when raising children in the faith. The main problem occurs when too many groups and organizations must integrate their agendas into lessons. Yet they don't consider whether children benefit from said lessons or if the teaching is more about honoring a specific policy or ideology. There is a significant problem with groups like these, which essentially involve children who can't contribute to their cause and have an irrational belief that their teaching somehow contributes to a safer, more tolerant, and more accepting world. This assumption is gravely inaccurate, given that teenagers have a still-limited capacity to form attitudes and beliefs in a fully informed manner before the age of 16. Many teens must turn 18 or 19 to develop confident, fully informed attitudes and beliefs.

This is not to say that prosocial engagement is somehow harmful to teens. Schools should motivate children to do sports, practice philanthropy, and productively help their communities. But when a school aims to affect what your child believes in and when the information that the school is using to influence said beliefs is only loosely related to science and facts, parents are right to be concerned. Parents should be encouraged to be open and honest with schools and vocal about the fact that they expect the school to benefit their child and not the other way around. It is important to have grace and love when speaking to teachers since many of them are trying their best to be cautious about the content of their lesson plans and have anxiety about complaints from parents.

Nevertheless, schools have one primary purpose. That purpose is to provide the child with the necessary education and to equip them with critical thinking skills for an independent life and participation in their community. Anything beyond that is up for debate. Parents have every right to be concerned about the content of lessons in schools. Policy fads are integrated into curricula without sufficient research and verification. Some schools are quick to decide that a view or a piece of knowledge is valuable and necessary, even without any measurable and quantifiable evidence. Ultimately, when you're in a situation where the school teaches your child something you don't want them to learn or participate in, you ought to intervene. The argument for that is relatively straightforward: If, in theory, you have the right to homeschool your child, entirely shaping their worldview, why wouldn't you have their right to decide what your child learns at school? Many students are struggling more than ever before with the basic subjects of math, history, language arts, and science. Students are still having to catch up academically post-pandemic all while dealing with mental health issues, loss of loved ones, stress at home due to financial issues, or a parent's loss of a job. It's unfortunate that less time in school is devoted to the primary subjects and more to political ideologies or sexually explicit content. Some schools may expect students and their parents to tolerate these theories and ideologies but won't allow students to challenge them in the classroom or opt-out. For example, students and teachers can be reprimanded for not using the name or pronoun preferred by another student. This is the problem because educational institutions should not dictate how students should think. Rather they should teach them to observe all perspectives and ideas, think critically, and ask questions without fear of retaliation.

> "The philosophy of the schoolroom in one generation will be the philosophy of government in the next." – Abraham Lincoln

Christian schools can be expensive but are a better alternative to public schools if avoiding an anti-Christian education is a priority for you. Your teen can still benefit from a few years of a faith-based educational foundation. Even if your child attends a private Christian school, it is a parent's responsibility to be aware of what their child is learning since some nonbiblical teachings have made their way into teaching materials at private Christian schools.

Public schools seem convenient for parents, but that convenience comes at a cost. Common issues parents of public school students face go far beyond speculative origin theories or inappropriate lesson content. They encounter offensive library books, the risk of child safety in restrooms and locker rooms, an unfair sports competition for girls, and being shamed for praying at lunch. The most severe issue is that when parents discover something they attempt to discuss with the school, they face red tape or pushback due to state and federal laws that protect school policies. Parents can be better prepared and self-educated about their state's laws and policies before addressing concerns at the school. The downloadable guide called *Back To School For Parents* at familypolicyalliance.com/back-to-school-for-parents is an excellent and helpful resource to keep handy. It is a compelling guide that provides insight into what's happening in schools, parental rights, and how to advocate for your child.

The information schools have on children has been increasing over the years. There is some information that a school should have on your child so that they're able to provide them with better care and attention. They should know about your child's talents, strengths, weaknesses, health, and background. With this information, teachers can adjust your child's lessons and learning materials and provide them with the needed help.

Some schools have very tricky policies regarding talking to students and interviewing them with or without parental knowledge. Before you sign your child into a school, check their policies to see how teachers and counselors communicate with students and which protocols they've set to keep you notified about who gets to talk to your child. Many parents worry about counselors, psychologists, and other staff getting too involved in their families and personal lives. In some situations, it's justified for schools to be kept in the loop with things that go on at home. Some families go through changes or tragedies that impose the need for the school to provide the child with extra support. But what happens if your child is interviewed and asked about their preferred pronouns and if they would like to try hormone therapy without your knowledge? Many schools seek out this type of information under the guise of protecting students from discrimination when actually, they are confusing students and violating parental rights. Some states don't require parental consent for schools to include the child in gender-related activities. For example, some schools in Arizona actively promote online chat rooms run by non-professional volunteers and without parental consent for students as young as 10 years of age to question their gender and sexuality. The list of things schools are obliged to notify parents about is getting shorter and shorter every year.

The number of gender identities and definitions continues to increase and is expected to evolve and be endless. Some schools in some states have begun integrating sexual orientation and gender identity into their lessons, even if not rooted in science. Ask questions if you see "non-binary" or any of these gender terms on your child's school forms. There are several concerns to focus on in this regard:

First, many people are uncomfortable with schools evading the scientific facts that men and women each have their role in procreation and the increasing evidence that medical and other interventions that cut across this are deeply problematic and harmful. Schools also hide relevant information, like extremely high suicide rates among transgender teens that have undergone transition, mainly because it's irreversible.

Secondly, students and parents are not allowed to question the narrative. Selective teaching, meaning biased education that only uses information that supports a particular narrative, is used. Any information that advocates for an opposing view is either ignored or disregarded. This form of manipulation with information rids parents of their right and grounds to opt their children out of these programs. If any of the lesson plans oppose values and attributes such as individuality, freedom, critical thinking, or asking questions without pushback, this could be a red flag.

Although sex education is designed to help students protect their health and have more agency over their bodies, statistics paint a different picture. Sexual education programs have a high failure rate. Almost 85% of these programs fail to provide the education they aim to deliver and instead encourage teenagers to enter sexual relationships.

In addition, if a school cultivates strong support for the LGBTQ community, they may allow transgender females into girls' private spaces, like bathrooms and locker rooms. This policy can make many girls feel unsafe. Girls sometimes feel disrespect when disadvantaged, such as when transgender girls are allowed to compete in the same teams as biological girls; these transgender girls also have a biological advantage when it comes to winning at sports. The same is true for boys, who might feel uncomfortable sharing their private spaces with biological girls.

The matters of sex and gender are not the only ones troubling parents in schools. The liberal approach to children's upbringing also means that your child could come across books and teaching materials that you'd find inappropriate, thanks to the freedom given to staff members to make their own choices regarding content to display. Although schools are generally committed to maintaining age-appropriate content in their classrooms, the interpretation of what's age-appropriate can differ from teacher to teacher and from librarian to librarian. It is reasonable to assume that any organization or content creator may obtain permission to distribute materials in schools if their content fits a particular framework (e.g., no explicit violence, nudity, or inappropriate language in the said content). However, schools often need more time or resources to run thorough background checks on everyone they engage with. Still, they are under pressure to provide a variety of educational experiences. The bottom line is schools can be careless about the values and implicit messages within content that is allowed in classrooms, which is vital to consider as a parent.

The notion that children should have the autonomy to determine their sexual orientation and gender identity is dangerous. Having this autonomy could mean they can, at any point, also claim they have the autonomy to subject themselves to hormone-blocking procedures and irreversible surgeries or, arguably just as bad, to be in a relationship with older adults. Remember, children's brains are not yet developed enough to make permanent life-changing decisions. Therefore, children need their parents to identify and talk about the sources of immoral influences with them. Explain to your child why certain content, lessons, and popular habits are corrupt and the potential spiritual and health repercussions of these things. Explain the biblical view that God assigns only two genders (male and female) as shown in the Bible and that affirming a false gender is not loving but is, in fact, a lie and a disservice to the other person.

The second thing you can do is carefully examine and study the school's policies and practices. Read the fine print on documents and permission slips. Review the homework assignments and books your child brings home and the content on the school intranet if your child accesses it from home. Look for any history, biology, math, or other lesson content that is questionable. Point out these inaccuracies with your child and discuss with them how they are invalid. Check if reading assignments are appropriate. Some parents have made a sacrifice to move so that their child can attend a different school where their child can perform better and where the school policies are aligned with their values.

Try to form a good relationship with teachers and school staff. Talk to your child's teachers and share your concerns. Go over the curricula, internet usage, protocol against bullying, and medical policies and procedures. Inform yourself of your rights. Engage with the school board and PTA meetings where you can advocate for your children. Refer to the *Family Policy Alliance* website for resources on parental and student rights in your state to be prepared.

Don't be afraid of being judged or mocked. Instead, pray for your child, their teachers, and God's intervention and guidance. Remember, the harmful influences imposed on children come from unverified schools of thought whose primary purpose is to spread a philosophy, not necessarily to educate. Plus, chances are that many parents, even those who don't identify with any faith or religion, agree with you. They simply don't want to stand out or have their children called out for not being progressive enough.

Homeschooling allows lessons to be customized to accommodate your child's learning pace and learning style. The lessons can also be customized around your calendar and work schedule. It's an opportunity to meet other parents and your child to socialize with like-minded children. The chance to know your child on a deeper level and see their strengths and passions firsthand are also benefits. Homeschooling parents also swap teaching each other's kids and collaborate on ideas. According to the *Home School Legal Defense Association,* costs can start from $50 per student, depending on how resourceful you are, or go up to $500 per student if extras, such as tutors, online courses, and sports, are included.

God's plan for education, at least for the Israelites in the Bible, was for the parents to educate their children directly. So, wouldn't it be the same for those today who wish to live according to God's will? One of the most profound scriptures in the Bible on education is "Hear, Israel! The Lord is our God, the Lord is one! And you shall love the Lord your God with all your heart and with all your soul and with all your strength. These words, which I am commanding you today, shall be on your heart. And you shall repeat them diligently to your sons and speak of them when you sit in your house, when you walk on the road, when you lie down, and when you get up. You shall also tie them as a sign to your hand, and they shall be as frontlets on your forehead. You shall also write them on the doorposts of your house and on your gates (New American Standard Version Bible, 2020, Deut. 6:4-9)

Consider the homeschool option if you have the time or flexibility with work-from-home accommodations. You are very qualified since you are the one who cares more about your child than anyone else. There are so many books, blogs, homeschool communities, and organizations to provide support. A good resource for information can be found on the *Family Policy Alliance* website. The *Home School Legal Defense Association* website is another one.

This world and culture may not change much for the better, but you may be able to help with how your child responds to it. If your child's future is important to you in this way, step five to an improved parent-teen relationship is talking to your child about what they are learning at school. Then look into the quality of your child's education and the environment. Get involved at the school and adjust if necessary. Pray and have conversations with teachers and other parents. Share this book with at least one family. If it revived your faith, your desire to seek God's will for your family, and the desire to the right thing, and if you would like to see other families enjoy God's blessings as well, share your thoughts about it in a review! It may help a parent who is struggling in this area and needs encouragement to consider this book.

6

MIND, BODY AND SPIRIT

We know that intrusive technology, media, groups, and the education system are not the only culprits for the negative impact on raising teens. Your child's behavior, performance, and mood depend on how well they do in mind, body, and spirit. Teenagers are extremely emotional and rebel, regress, and throw tantrums as a part of their development. Intellectually, teenagers are becoming more intelligent and capable of understanding new information and gaining new knowledge. Their personalities are also developing, and they are developing likes and dislikes, tastes and preferences, as well as complex personality and character traits. If you can get your teen to browse through one of their social media account feeds while sitting next to you, you'll have a general idea of what some of their interests and preferences are. Social media companies are subject matter experts in collecting this type of data. Teenagers also develop physically and physiologically faster than their intellectual and emotional maturation. Emotionally though, your teen is still your small child. They may not say it, but they still like it when you kiss them good night. If they didn't feel so rebellious, they would still enjoy napping next to you on the couch while you watch T.V. Even if your teenager is striving for independence, they still need parental attention and guidance as they mature.

Adults often forget just how big of a child a teenager is, even though they are just physically big. After all, seeing that they can do chores, handle age-appropriate responsibilities, serve their meals, and clean up afterward makes many parents think that their work is done. It's far from that. Their brains work a lot different than that of adults. Since their brain is still developing until their mid to late 20s, they will still act impulsively out of fear and not think about consequences. The amygdala part of the brain, which controls reaction and response, develops before the frontal cortex, which controls reasoning. In fully developed adult brains, this frontal cortex enables thinking before acting, whereas in teen brains, acting occurs before thinking. This is why parents must have patience, remind and repeat words of wisdom, and advise their teens in grace and with love. Still, allow them to face the consequences, and repetition is key. They will get it eventually. It's a delicate balance between giving them some leeway with certain things but if they don't respect the boundaries you've set, then cut back the privilege of that extra freedom until they can prove they are responsible.

They are still kids and want to have fun, so if you can find ways to distract them from their devices and provide more fun and real experiences, you are closer to keeping their attention and influencing them significantly. So, if your teen's interest is fashion, buy some oversized tees at the thrift store and redesign them with your teen by painting and cutting them. If their interest is music learn to play the guitar or any instrument together. If they have a new interest in bodybuilding, get some weights and work out together. Capturing your teen's attention with quality time will let them see you want to know them and value time with them. Take advantage of these moments to have conversations about school, friends, and favorite things. If tech companies spend fortunes capturing the attention of teens' eyes and ears, wouldn't you also see the value of it? It's like gold if you can leverage that knowledge to get their attention and influence their habits and behavior. These conversations can naturally become discussions about sex, drugs, and the harder things that should be discussed. Drugs and alcohol delay the development of the logical frontal cortex in teens, so when discouraging your teen from doing something, having reasons like this to explain to your teen why you don't want them to do it is a lot more effective than just restricting without explanation.

Having a strong, centered, stable structure for the kind of behavior you expect in your family helps your child internalize a moral structure of their own. Of course, no one is perfect, and God is always working on us and shaping us. Admitting in front of them that you, too, cope with temptation and failure but always strive toward honoring God in your daily words and actions will strengthen your child's faith in you and God. Demonstrate self-control in stressful situations. When your child gets emotional about something, pray and try to stay composed with self-control. Over time you will get better at it, and your teen will see that emotional outbursts are ineffective and will not trigger you. They will seek to model after you in this way.

Respectable publications on the psychology of raising teens attest that spiritual and more conservative households instill more guidance and security than free-range parenting.

The research found that most children's behavior depends on the bond they share with their parents. This concept is easily explained with attachment theory, which groups parent-child relationships into one of four categories: safe, anxious, dismissive, and fearful. In a safe or secure relationship, the child has a strong role model in their parents. The bond between them is profound and includes sharing fears and insecurities and finding support in learning healthy ways to cope with life's hurdles. The trick with attachment theory is that it warns us that only a secure connection can be considered healthy. The secure connection is most related to positive outcomes for children, while the remaining three correlate with developing anxiety, depression, and behavioral problems. All other connections result from parental coldness, negligence, and abuse.

Similarly, when our teens and we have a strong bond with God as our heavenly Father, we have a secure sense of identity in Him as our Rock, our Fortress. This identity makes a developing child less likely to be swayed or influenced because of the solid spiritual foundation in Christ.

Here is another point where faith and psychology meet. Parents are the main culprits for their child's behavior. In the same way, you get to be proud of your children's virtue and achievement, and you also share the responsibility for their bad behavior. We see this in the example of Eli in the Bible, who, alongside his sons, is punished by God for their transgressions and misuse of their authority as priests as accounted for in 1 Samuel 2:12. The Lord disciplines not only Eli's sons but also Eli himself since the way he brought up his sons determined their behavior. His sons abused their power in the community because they weren't taught to be humble and honor God. More importantly, they disrespected God.

Now reflect on some of your child's mischief. If your child has ever gotten into a fight, stolen, or engaged in immoral activities, who did they disrespect the most? Perhaps you're angry that they embarrassed you with their tantrum or threw a fit. The fact that there are natural consequences to said behaviors is of reasonable but minor importance compared to how the entire family disrespected God. But why the whole family?

Let's say your child felt enticed by your neighbor's assets, so they stole something from their home or shed. Theft is a direct violation of the commandment, "You shall not steal" (New American Standard Version Bible, 2020, Exodus 20:15), and should be a bigger worry than what the neighbor will think. A child's biggest betrayal is against honesty and love for their neighbor—in other words, against God. Shall they repent, they are to do so in a way that expresses love and humility to their neighbor and God directly and indirectly. However, let's take a closer look at what caused this behavior. Why was your child so heavily enticed in the first place, and why did they show so little restraint?

The answer to the first question lies in your relationship with your child. Children often misbehave to draw attention to themselves. Sometimes parents are caught up in their own problems, but also, some families only provide negative attention. The child is ignored when they are doing well and is not receiving any reward, love, or praise for it. However, when they misbehave, their parents start paying more attention to them. Other times, mischief is a cry for help. Your child may want you to think about how they're doing and feeling. They want you to be more involved.

The second reason some teens show little restraint when regulating feelings and resisting peer pressure is not having internalized boundaries. A child needs to have a sense of boundaries, to be told what they can and can't do, and not to be allowed to get away with mischief. Indeed, some of our children's misconduct can be endearing, but we don't brush it off easily. Think about the consequences of the child's action if they began to repeat that same behavior in a different setting and with other people. Are you noticing how a seemingly funny act of taking a photo with a fake cigarette while standing in front of a no-smoking sign is just to make his family laugh? What if, the next time they did it, trying to make friends laugh, they used a real cigarette in front of a no-smoking sign at school where the campus cop was nearby? This scenario is the exact kind of sweet trap that the enemy sets for parents. Minor mischief, barely enough to make you notice warning signs, can cause much trouble.

Sadly, free-range parenting is becoming more popular. It is an incorrect response to mainstream teachings of the need to respond to children's needs and empathize. Any child psychologist would tell you that boundaries are essential for a child. They are pillars that build a moral compass and enable the child to make their own decisions and judgments. As general recommendations, boundaries should be reasonable, clear, achievable, and, more importantly, consistent. List everything a child is and isn't allowed to do and commit to maintaining said boundaries as best as possible.

God has entrusted you with your children, so as long as they are under your roof, they are your responsibility. Nevertheless, try to avoid carrying the burden by yourself. Rely on God's Word, family, and close, trusted friends for prayer and professional faith-based counseling.

Multiple scriptures in the Bible establish parental authority and instruct children to obey their parents so they can have a long life. In that regard, you are an image to which the child shapes their behavior regarding strengths and weaknesses. Parents are too quick to judge that it's the school or the street that corrupted a child. Ask any teacher, and they will tell you that each student in their classroom is a lively image of their family. This is not to disregard the negative influences from the environment and culture. They are absolutely there. However, the child's susceptibility to those influences, the manner and intensity to which the child will fall under peer pressure, and the degree to which they will be able to correct their behavior also comes from their home. Your child will emulate how you speak, act, and respond to situations. If you want your child to adhere to biblical standards, ask God to help you model godly characteristics.

God's children should look to Him in striving to live righteously because His righteousness in us is good since we are not good on our own. Many believe they are "good" because they are kind, courteous, thoughtful, and loving to those who treat them kindly. So, is being "good" good enough? In the U.S., there's much diversity regarding raising children, and the social climate is less favorable than in Nordic countries.

Now, let's address one crucial paradox. Despite having an entirely liberal legal and philosophical frame, Nordic societies are much more traditional and conservative than societies in the U.S. On the surface, people have very few limitations regarding lifestyle and choices. However, these countries have the lowest crime, suicide, and mental illness rates, at least regarding children. These cultures can be described as minimalistic, with a high emphasis on prosocial values. Children are given all the reasonable freedom, but they seem to have little interest in exercising it. Have you ever wondered why? Such social climates as those in Nordic countries have a low tolerance for immoral behaviors, and the entire system is set up to provide moral guidance for children. It appears to be working well, for now at least, that the population doesn't need social norms that prescribe living according to the Bible's teachings. If God is absent from this culture, where do they get their values?

Although many of these people do not practice a religion or claim to be believers, their heritage is a God-fearing culture. Some claim that many years ago, because these countries had a state church, the values they have today are rooted in the belief in God from prior generations. It may be that these values have just been passed on down from generation to generation, but there is still a void. Living with good values is nice for living in peace, but what happens after death? At their core, people want to know the truth about their identity, their purpose, and what happens after death. When your teen is secure in knowing they are a child of God, their purpose is to live for God, and that they have a place in heaven for eternity after death, they will be much more content than simply being virtuous but wandering without purpose. The third chapter in the book of Romans mentions that no one is good, and all have sinned. We are forgiven and promised eternal life after death, not on merit but because of God's grace and mercy when he died for us, for our sins. He died for your children too. Therefore, it's essential to show grace to your children and not expect perfection. The Bible says, "For by grace you have been saved through faith; and this is not of yourselves, it is the gift of God; not of works, so that no one may boast." (New American Standard Version Bible, 2020, Ephesians 2: 8-9) They will fall at times, and that's okay. They will learn from their mistakes. Most important above good behavior is a repentant heart and relationship with God.

Mutual love and respect between family members are the foundation for raising a healthy child. A give-and-take approach to your relationships with family members is important. Give respect, and you can expect the same in return. When the environment within your home is loving, accepting, and respectful, your child will take what they learn to school and everywhere they go. A good practice some families have is meeting regularly, at least once a week, together in one room without electronic devices to share struggles they are having and to pray together. This family gathering opens the door to showing compassion and respect. Your child's physical, mental, and spiritual health depends on the quality of their lifestyle, sleep, and food, as well as their home environment and relationships.

Health is a prerequisite to the child's development, and it is also a prerequisite for a family living in peace with God. Thank God for doctors and modern medicine, but healthcare is proactively caring for your child's health to prevent disease. Diet has a significant influence on children's behavior. Let's look at how your child's diet affects their mood, energy, and ability to focus and learn.

For a child to behave well, they first need to be feel well. To feel well, they need to be fed well. Nowadays, children mostly eat food saturated with chemicals and processed sugars. This type of food affects their mood negatively, both directly and indirectly. Unhealthy food hurts your child's digestive health directly by destroying beneficial intestinal flora, leaving their intestines passable. Without good healthy intestinal flora to filter harmful toxins and bacteria, a reasonable degree of harmful substances from the food reaches the bloodstream and, consequently, the brain. There, toxic substances from food can hurt the child's natural development. Their immune system becomes overactive to prevent bacteria and toxins from causing permanent harm. All of this combined leads to an imbalance in the child's brain chemistry. Both children and adults on an unhealthy diet exhibit nervousness, unstable and depressive moods, and problems with healthy sleep. Your child's body, under these circumstances, produces vast amounts of stress hormones, and in this case, the body is in distress. Parents often don't know that too much cortisol in the child's blood can directly inhibit healthy growth and development. Your child can miss out on the potential to be as strong, intelligent, and creative as they would with a healthy diet. Even worse, malnutrition is proven to connect with children's mental illnesses and contributes to numerous chronic diseases and behavioral disorders. Aside from the stress hormone cortisol, your child's body produces too much adrenaline from overeating sugar. Amid a sugar high, the child cannot rest, focus, or follow instructions. Their attention is scattered, and all they do is pursue the next source of excitement. Your child becomes more nervous and fidgety while their overactive immune system affects their mood as it declines further.

Now let's address how nutrition affects your child's behavior positively. Quality, nutrient-dense meals provide an abundance of healthy fats, protein, fiber, and micronutrients (vitamins and minerals). Macronutrients (healthy fats, protein, and complex carbs) fuel your child's energy while building the cells and tissues for their still-developing bodies. Micronutrients play a similar role; except they are significant in regulating hormones. Vitamins and minerals are absorbed in the gut and then used to create hormones that induce a cheerful, relaxed mood. When your child gets enough vitamins, their brain can produce more serotonin, endorphin, dopamine, and melatonin. These hormones enable the child to stay calm, cheerful, and focused.

When your child isn't getting enough vitamins, they can become nutrient deficient. In this state, they can become depressed, nervous, irritable, and fussy. Vitamins most commonly affecting children's moods include A, D, C, and B. While vitamin C can be obtained in sufficient amounts easily through common foods, the same can't be said for vitamins A, D, and B. Iron deficiency is most common in the U.S., despite high levels of meat consumption. According to Naturopathicpediatrics.com, milk can partially block the absorption of iron. Some medications can also block absorption of certain B vitamins and some minerals.

So, what are some simple steps to improve your child's nutrition? Here are a couple of food suggestions:

Magnesium and Zinc: These nutrients are found in dairy and root vegetables. Most people are deficient in magnesium, so avocados, cashews, dark chocolate, and pumpkin seeds are good sources of magnesium. Chuck roast, cashews, and Greek yogurt contain zinc. These nutrients support relaxation and nourish the nervous system, while zinc helps regulate melatonin and boosts the immune system. Melatonin supports healthy sleep, which means healthy growth and a happy mood. A melatonin supplement is discouraged since it is a hormone that the body produces naturally. Too much melatonin supplementation can cause sleep issues. The best approach is to have your child tested for any deficiencies.

Healthy Fats: The omega-3s found in fish and seafood support intellectual development as they nourish the brain. Studies showed that kids with adequate omega-3 intake averaged higher reading performance than those without sufficient levels. Olive oil and avocados are also good food for the brain.

Grains and Legumes for Vitamins B, D, and A - Quinoa, chia seeds, whole wheat, and rice are all great sources of these precious nutrients. Exercising 15 minutes daily in the sunshine will help boost vitamin D levels which is important for boosting the immune system, hormonal balance, and energy.

Leafy greens and cruciferous plants: Spinach, kale, and broccoli may not be the child's favorites, but they bring tons of micronutrients. They're rich in vitamin C, iron, potassium, fiber, and other essential nutrients.

Protein: Some of the best sources of protein are lamb, beef, sardines, eggs and white beans. These foods contain plenty of protein to help them with muscle and energy, and they also have micronutrients to match. Lean foods high in protein also include plenty of potassium and magnesium, which support immune and cardiovascular health. A smoothie with banana or blueberries, leafy greens, coconut oil, and a good-quality protein powder makes a quick, nutritious breakfast.

Adaptogenic herbs: Dr. Mark Sherwood, ND, recommends herbs like Ashwagandha, Rhodiola, Valerian, passionflower, and chamomile for reducing anxiety. He says it is sometimes necessary to be on medications but that with these medicinal herbs and nutritious foods God created and the body's natural healing mechanisms, healing can occur. One can be weaned off medications while working with a doctor for an exit strategy to help with this transition with no time frame.

Parents and teens both need to prioritize sleep. Poor sleep results in irritability and an inability to resolve conflict. Then, teens lose sleep due to escalated conflicts, even if it was just between the parents. Parents also have issues falling asleep if they conflict with each other or their teens. This may be a good reason the Bible says, "Be angry and do not sin; do not let the sun go down on your anger, and do not give the devil an opportunity." (New American Standard Version Bible, 2020, Ephesians 4:26-27). What you can do to help everyone at home get quality sleep is:

- Ask to pray with anyone in the family with whom you have had a conflict and forgive.

- Have everyone try to put the lights out for rest consistently every night at the same time.

- Minimize the use of blue light that comes from electronic devices before bed.

- Try to avoid working or studying all night.

- Try to block out time for tasks to get done more efficiently during the day to allow sleeping earlier.

- Try natural sleep aids such as cherry juice, valerian root, and magnesium glycinate.

- Avoid eating late at night, especially sugar and caffeine.

- Avoid exercise late at night before bed.

In 1879, William Beal planted seeds in 20 bottles to test how long they could survive. Every 20 years, his team would dig up a bottle to check whether the seeds had germinated.

After 142 years, many seeds contained in these bottles had sprouted. They outlived the researcher and many other people, for that matter. All they had was soil and God.

Every time you plant a seed by praying with your teen or sharing a scripture, you sow an investment into their life. It may not come to fruition right away. You can expect that they may act like they're ignoring you or that there was no direct impact on them. However, someday, with continued prayer and patience, you may find that those seeds show fruit later in their lives. Child development experts also attest that each parental intervention takes at least several months to show progress, often much longer. The more you seed, the more you encourage your child to live according to the Bible, and the stronger and more powerful that seed inside them grows.

Peace is necessary to get rest, and according to Dr. Avery Johnson (Johnson, 2021), there is a difference between sleeping and resting. Just because you're sleeping doesn't mean you're resting. Think of thoughts and words as self-proclaiming prophecies. Your brain analyzes all the information about your experiences throughout the day and then adjusts your body to react accordingly. The more you worry, the more your body is stressed. This state of stress also affects your spirit. Sadly, while you worry, you're distancing yourself from God as you prioritize worry over faith in God. Dr. Avery states that one in five kids has a diagnosable mental health condition, such as depression, anxiety, ADHD, and behavior disorders linked to these looping thoughts. Words are powerful, and parents must be careful not to criticize their teens publicly. Even in private, parents must choose their words carefully and be tactful when providing feedback and correction to their teen. Always be truthful and genuine. Build up with words and avoid tearing down their spirit. "There is one who speaks rashly like the thrusts of a sword, but the tongue of the wise brings healing" (New American Standard Version Bible, 2020, Prov. 12:18). The first few verses in chapter 15 of Proverbs also provide wisdom on the power of the tongue.

You can help protect your child from toxic thoughts by speaking the truth to them (Clarke, 2016). Do so by teaching your child they are valuable and made in God's image. Avoid excessive praise as much as toxic criticism. Provide encouraging, uplifting feedback, the kind of helpful feedback that is moderate and healthy for your child. An excellent place to start a conversation is on a positive note, something good you observe about them and then tactfully provide correction in love. It could sound like, "Son, you are so much smarter than those guys causing trouble. I love you too much to see them drag you down a destructive path. They are not true friends if they don't respect your decision to quit the bad behavior. Let's pray for God to provide new friends."

Now, let's discuss unified parenting. You and your spouse are a team—if not your spouse, then your co-parent. Often, we prioritize what we want and consider our desires so important that we lose sight of how much unity and consistency children require. If you and the child's other parent clash regarding attitudes, your child will also experience inner conflict. You and the co-parent may not see eye to eye on everything, so try to pray, ask God for direction, and to change the co-parent's heart in those instances. Try to reach a middle ground that serves your child's best interest. Suppose the child goes back and forth between two households without cooperation from the co-parent. In that case, the only thing you can do is have consistency in routines and expectations in your own home and have patience and understanding as your child has to adapt and adjust from one parenting style to another.

Are you aware of spiritual oppression, and are you and your family protecting yourselves from it? Occasionally, occult influences lie hidden in games and so-called fun practices that we wouldn't think much about.

Let's take an example of one of the most common mental illnesses: depression. There's a story in The Christian Post of a well-meaning medium, Jenn Nizza, who engaged in tarot readings, thinking she was helping people communicate with deceased loved ones (Hallowell, 2022). However, her practices hurt her the most, and soon after engaging in occult practices, she started getting sick. She suffered from an eating disorder and eventually suffered from depression so severe that it almost ruined her life. It wasn't before she almost hit rock bottom that this young woman finally prayed to Christ to deliver her from evil. Jesus showed up for her, and she now dedicates her life to speaking up against the dangers of New Age spiritualism and the occult.

Ask yourself if your family members have, consciously or unconsciously, engaged in occult activities. Additionally activities such as New Age spiritual practices, watching horror movies, watching pornography, doing yoga, and other practices invite demonic influences. Although some experiences, like abuse and molestation, can't be put in the same category as the previous, they can create such stress as to open doors for all sorts of intrusion. Seek deliverance and repentance for actions taken, and you will see an overall improvement in your family's spiritual health. Deliverance is a term that, biblically speaking, means to be liberated and rescued from evil spiritual oppression or bondage through God's promises. Read more about this in chapter 7: Virtuous Attributes.

When teens do not have a strong sense of self and are perceived as weak or vulnerable, they become easy targets for drug pushers and bullies. They may portray confidence around you, but in a social circle, they try hard not to look like a "loser" and ignore their conscience just to fit in. However, the child doesn't even need, for example, to consciously take drugs to fall into the terrible vice of drug addiction. A naive teen accepts "candy," "drinks," or a substance from a stranger. They overdose instantly and end up either in a coma or dying from the intake. Every so often, look up commonly abused drugs and share with your child what they look like so they can avoid them. Other types of peer pressure are theft and sexual activity. As awkward as it may be, it's worth letting your teen hear these talks from you rather than outsiders. If they are informed and warned by their parent first, they are much less likely to fall into a trap. Also, keep an eye out for signs like a change in their demeanor, bruises, black eyes, or anything unusual or out of character so you can immediately seek medical attention and report abuse to authorities.

A good defense against these risks includes your teen having a solid identity in Christ and knowing God's Word. Therefore, investing time together in Bible study together is valuable. They are awesomely and wonderfully made, as stated in Psalms 139:14. Point out to your child all the good character traits they have and how they make them beautiful more than physical traits. Even if your child is not yet receptive to God and Bible scriptures, bonding in your relationship is crucial. Build up your child's self-esteem by sharing what God says about them and reassuring them of their worth based on their character rather than their appearance or abilities. Even the most attractive popular kid at their school could be so rude to people that it makes them unattractive to everyone. A few different approaches for your teen to stand up to bullies are:

Ignoring the bully – The bully is looking for a reaction. If your teen walks off in another direction and acts like they didn't hear what the bully said, the bully may back off.

Interrupt the bully mid-sentence – If your teen can be assertive, they can cut off the bully assertively mid-sentence, saying, for example, "John! Enough! Stop!"

Laugh it off with the bully – If your teen feels secure in themselves, they can laugh as if it's no big deal and downplay it as if they both have the same sense of humor. Again, this does not give the bully the satisfaction of winning. It goes both ways.

Always be with a friend(s) – When your teen has a friend or group of friends to stick with them, the bully is less likely to be a bother.

Avoid the bully – Your teen can try to take note of where the bully usually hangs out and stay away as much as possible.

Teach your child to be a peacemaker and comforter if their friend or classmate is bullied. Opening your home to invite your teen's friends while you're there allows you to get to know who they are and then facilitate conversations with your teen about those friends. Could you get to know their parents too? The more time spent with their friends and their parents, the easier it will be to decide if you are comfortable allowing your teen to participate in a sleepover or to let them drive the car to ride with friends. Getting involved in the details of their life while at other times giving them space is a balancing act, but worth it.

Bullying is any repeated hurtful behavior on a weaker individual, and this can be verbal or physical and using intimidation. It also includes being touched in unwanted and inappropriate ways, which is physical abuse. In many cases, the offenders are people the child knows, like teachers, coaches, relatives, or even juvenile offenders (age 12 and up, of which 93% are boys). Protect your teens by being aware of any grooming photos or texts on your child's phone or school device. Meet and talk to other parents and school staff about sexual abuse awareness. Ensure that your child goes to safe places where they complete thorough background checks and screenings on all adults and staff. Lastly, pray over them for protection and be available to them, constantly reassuring your child that he/she can talk to you about anything bothering them. Furthermore, remind them to keep boundaries when it comes to their body.

Compassion is one of the most admirable human qualities. To teach a child to be compassionate first requires teaching them that we are all God's creation and created equally. From others in third world countries to neighbors right next to us, people suffer and sometimes silently. Teach your child that the world does not revolve around them, but that God designed us to love our neighbor, be the salt on the earth, and be light in the darkness. A pastor once said in his sermon, "for many people, your presence is your present." So, remind your child that just as he enjoys having friends come to his birthday party and having visitors on occasion, it's equally important to take the time and be present for others, including relatives, the elderly, patients in the hospital, orphans, and widows as they might need help and prayer.

Compassion requires us to emulate how God sees us in our sinful nature. We all have sinned at some point, but He has mercy and sympathizes with us. We should also be sympathetic and love those who act up by praying for them and showing care through our actions. There is hope for everyone! Just like He called out Saul, who persecuted Christians in the Bible, and converted him to serve God, God can take the most wicked criminal and save him from sin. A good scripture to support this is "Bear one another's burdens, and thereby fulfill the law of Christ." (New American Standard Version Bible, 2020, Gal. 6:2)

God created the institution of marriage between a husband and wife, as stated in Matthew 19 of the Bible. Mutual care and respect for one another create the safety zone for your child that they need desperately. However, how are you supposed to have a healthy marriage in faith if you're stressed out and suffering from unresolved marital issues? Remember, your children are watching and learning from your relationships. They learn how to manage stress, resolve conflict, and pick themselves up after difficult experiences. Your children are looking at you when learning how to resolve conflict. The more stress and toxicity there is in your marriage or co-parent relationship, the more your children learn to resolve arguments through power struggles, selfishness, vanity, and insults. Don't allow this to happen! Look at how you communicate and resolve conflicts in all of your relationships. Try to avoid yelling in front of your children. You and your spouse can demonstrate healthy listening and communication skills and the ability to compromise.

All family members are connected. You cannot have an isolated traumatic or stressful experience without it affecting everyone. Yes, stress is toxic for children, quite literally. Stress can delay cerebral development. It can harm your child's immune health and cause them to become increasingly ill, and you also know that it can open the door to spiritual oppression. So, what are you to do to manage stress in everyday life?

If your child is withdrawn, melancholic, uninterested in playing and studying, and is beginning to underperform at school, it could be a sign that they're coping with stress.

In some cases, the stress comes from having too much burden at school and having unrealistic expectations set for them. Other stressors could be changes in their body, illness, problems with friends, not measuring up to their peers, or confusion about life. Are you and your spouse arguing frequently? All of these can be potential reasons for a child to begin suffering from stress. If unattended, stress can lead to illnesses, anxiety, and depression. Sometimes, you'll be going through a rough patch and won't have the strength to be content or patient. These difficulties can result from illness and trauma; you're not to blame.

However, it would help if you employed these recommended techniques for your entire family to heal from stress:

- Pray both individually and as a family.
- Reassure your child that God is in control and can be trusted.
- Attend church, read scriptures, and do your best to live by the Bible.
- Spend meaningful time together and bond with your family as much as possible.
- Support your child in expressing their feelings through conversation, play, or art.
- Get suitable therapy for any condition or trauma.
- Focus on good things to be thankful for.

Paying attention to your child's mental, physical, and spiritual health is the sixth step. Although none of these areas should be neglected, God should take precedence, so relationships with God and family should be a priority.

7

VIRTUOUS ATTRIBUTES

Bringing up your child is more than providing food, shelter, and education. Cultivating the virtues encouraged in the Bible are key to raising a teen who intentionally strives to live with moral excellence and have a positive impact on others. The Bible advises in Romans 12:2 not to be conformed to this world but to be transformed with a renewed mind. This is something all should practice throughout life since we are human and fail at times. God is constantly molding and shaping us like clay, and you can witness God doing this in your teen's life as well. As a God-fearing parent, one of your concerns is to model wisdom, godly character, and confidence for your child. Most parents are very busy especially parents who are single and working two jobs, just trying to provide all the basics: sports equipment, doctor co-pays, dental work, glasses, and all the other expenses for raising teens. This struggle is prevalent and not just understandable but admirable when a parent sacrifices so much of themselves to provide for their children. They may have little time to spare at the end of each day, but that little time is like gold and can go a long way if used wisely. Parents sometimes don't realize until it's too late that they only had a short time with their children under their roof before they're gone. The time you have to influence your child is so brief that it is wise to make the most of it. You only get one chance. Even if it's just half an hour in the evening, your child's heart and mind are more important than a messy house or stack of junk mail. Here are some practical ways of modeling virtues and imparting wisdom that builds virtuous character.

#1: Financial Stewardship

Most parents probably believe that teaching their children money management skills is sufficient. While this is true, a small lesson regarding the biblical view on money will go a long way and shape their financial future for years to come. According to God's Word, everything we have, even if we work for it, belongs to God, for He is the Creator of everything we have in the first place. "The earth is the Lord's and all it contains, the world and those who live in it." (New American Standard Version Bible, 2020, Ps. 24:1). He gives us the resources, the hands to work, and the mind to be creative. Since He is ultimately our provider, everything we have is a gift from God, and therefore we should give thanks and use it to God's glory. Allowing your teens to earn their own money helps them discover talents, skills, and passions they have. As tempting as it is to shower them with gifts sometimes, it is to their benefit to allow them to earn their own money to buy the extra luxuries they desire. It will help them understand the principles of working ethically and honestly within boundaries. A true story to illustrate this is about Oscar, brilliantly buying candy bars while they were on sale at the store and reselling them on his high school campus at lunchtime. He was making a nice little profit and was so proud of himself until, one day, he got caught by the school principal, who advised him that selling food items on campus was against the rules. The temptation to outsmart the principal and continue selling candy in a sneaky manner to make more money was greater than his desire to respect his authorities at school. So again, he got caught, suspended from school, and when his parents found out, he was grounded. Although his innovative idea could be applauded, he needed to face the consequence. After that, he was encouraged to pursue his sales skills off-campus.

Teaching them to manage money is an entirely different skill than earning it. Even many famous people, who possess wealth that measure millions of dollars, touch the depths of bankruptcy when they don't manage their money correctly. Take the time to read scriptures on wisdom about money with your teen. God is our provider, and we should not depend on money for happiness. Monetary wealth should not be an end goal. Instead, we should view money as a tool to care for our families and multiply it to invest in God's kingdom out of a cheerful heart by taking some of what God has given us and giving it to others in need.

Suppose you are in debt; model financial responsibility to your children by setting up a budget of income and expenses and paying off small debts first, working up toward the more significant debts or paying down the debts with higher interest rates. Develop a plan and get the family involved in living below your means by cutting back on unnecessary expenses. All these little things combined can provide financial relief and decrease stress.

Modeling financial stewardship that pleases God will make an invaluable impression on your teen.

More importantly, giving children opportunities to make their own money and then teaching them how to budget shows your child how to be content and prolong instant gratification. Here are some important considerations for teaching teens money management skills through the lens of faith:

Being grateful for our money and giving thanks to God is the first step toward financial stewardship. When teens can earn money by babysitting, house sitting, mowing lawns, watering plants, or walking dogs, they begin to have a greater appreciation for money and are more likely to have gratitude that honors God. If they do their work well, working as if God is their boss, they may be surprised to receive extra money or tips for an exceptional job. Believers should remember that they represent God when they work and should strive for excellence in their work with humility and gratitude. Model this attitude of gratitude for your child as much as you can.

The modern era is about overspending, shallow ambitions, and false impressions. People post photoshopped images of luxury apartments and cars on social media, but they're probably in serious debt. It appears younger generations are both fierce earners and merciless overspenders, and you can help your child become the first but not the latter. Support your child in resisting the temptation to spend. They don't have to have all the latest fads and spend the way everyone else spends. No matter how much your family earns, a lifestyle rid of financial pressure is only possible if one spends less than one makes. Encourage delayed gratification by staying at home or inviting friends over rather than going out, being mindful about spending fuel, and taking good care of their clothes, so they don't have to buy replacements. An excellent way to teach this to your child is when they are considering buying something, tell them to ask themselves the questions, "Is this something that is going to bring long-lasting value or provide a return on my investment?" and "Is this expense ultimately going to honor God to some degree?" If so, then encourage them to proceed!

Our material possessions have values that can be realistic, overestimated, or underestimated. Your child likely has an idea about what they want, but they should also be mindful of value. Many criteria determine value:

- how long an item will last

- how precious a trip is for them

- whether there is a long- or short-term benefit to purchasing

- whether they're just shopping on a whim or intentionally

Teach the child mindful spending in contemplating the value each purchase has for them. For example, your daughter might want a $100 pair of jeans. The product is of supreme quality, but is the brand name driving the price? The quality of the material of two different brands might be the same, providing the same value but varying greatly in price because of the brand. On that, your daughter can get a relatively affordable $40 pair of jeans that look the same. She could even buy a second pair of lower-cost jeans or put the rest in savings.

Show your child how to evaluate assets and how to project future value. Most assets either gain or lose value with time. You can find excellent sources online that show how certain assets change value over the years, which further helps demonstrate the value of your child's purchases. Experts in financial advice say that people should put their money more toward items that gain value in time (e.g., art, antiques, silver coins) instead of those things that lose value with time, such as cars and clothing. God is in favor of us buying physical assets that serve us well for living; however, it's good to remind your teen that what we spend our money on mainly reveals the attitude of our hearts. Matthew 6:19 in the Bible says that we shouldn't store up treasures on earth but instead store them up in heaven. Giving into what counts eternally is better than just living for the present things on earth, which are only temporary.

#2: Self-Control and Patience

"A gentle answer turns away wrath, but a harsh word stirs up anger. The tongue of the wise makes knowledge pleasant, but the mouth of the fools sprouts foolishness.". (New American Standard Version Bible, 2020, Prov. 15:1)

Have you ever caught yourself scolding your child and then scolding yourself on the inside for knowing that you're not achieving anything? Many parents have experienced such a moment when they are lashing out at their teenager and feel a gap forming between them, realizing that the angry words spoken are backfiring. But how are you supposed to react when your child pushes your buttons and tests your patience day after day?

This topic can be controversial as various parenting styles, and theories range from one extreme to the other regarding scolding and spanking, which can be confusing. Let's review what the Bible has to say about scolding. We know that yelling and harsh negative scolding don't help when it is venting in anger. On the one hand, the Bible tells fathers in Ephesians 6:4 not to provoke anger in their children but to raise them in the discipline and instruction of the Lord. However, the big question is, what is discipline? Is it physical punishment or a timeout? Do either of these even work on a teenager? There is a Proverb that says, "The rod and a rebuke give wisdom, but a child who gets his own way brings shame to his mother." (New American Standard Version Bible, 2020, Prov. 29:15), and another scripture says, "Do not withhold discipline from a child; though you strike him with the rod, he will not die.

"You shall strike him with the rod and rescue his soul from Sheol." (New American Standard Version Bible, 2020, Proverbs 23: 13-14). (Sheol is hell). Many parenting experts state that this scripture is only metaphorical and that the Bible does not condone corporal punishment, but "rod" in Hebrew means "stick." Hence, yes, the Bible permits spanking. Nevertheless, spanking should by no means under any circumstance occur by an angry parent. Many children have suffered and died from abuse. Many children like Billy are damaged and traumatized from abuse. Billy's birth father abandoned him, and his stepfather repeatedly beat him with his fists as punishment for years. Although now Billy is recovering with God's help over time as a grown adult, it has cost him two failed marriages due to unresolved anger issues. A good picture of discipline with spanking looks like Mary's story. Mary loved eating lemon wedges. At 13, she was at a restaurant with her aunt Mindy. Aunt Mindy caught Mary sticking her hand in the empty glass of iced tea, trying to get the lemon wedge out of it. Aunt Mary slapped her wrist and told her to use a fork to retrieve the lemon from the glass. Mary embarrassingly took her hand out of the glass. That slap was a shock to her but an effective one, and it didn't kill her. Aunt Mindy explained, "You could get your hand stuck in that glass, and it's bad table manners." She never put her hand in a glass again.

Not every child requires spanking. Step away if a conflict escalates and give yourself time to blow off steam. Then reassess and pray. Depending on their personality, a warning may be sufficient. Others require more stern instruction in love. Pray to ask God to direct you to discipline your child or children individually. The main goal is to get the instruction message across. It may not take much, especially if they already have their conviction, in which case they may take it upon themselves to come to you with their errors and need for advice.

Additionally, your child can learn discipline from their mistakes. If parents always intervene to prevent that consequence, the child will not grow from it. Of course, at times, it may be necessary to intervene if the child can potentially hurt himself or hurt others. In other words, you, as a parent, should not take the burden of trying to control everything your teen does.

For example, you might not let your teen drive the family car if they are under strong medication after a wisdom tooth removal procedure. However, under normal circumstances, for most teens, a fender bender accident or a speeding ticket is inevitable during the first few years of driving. That is why their auto insurance premiums are so high. You cannot control that. Once they experience it, you can have them do extra chores or ask them to save money from their weekend job to help cover the cost of the insurance deductible, and hopefully, they will learn to be more careful drivers.

According to the National Library of Medicine, the behavioral and decision-making part of the brain is not fully developed until age 25. Parents need to have grace when their children make poor decisions, and they also need to put their children in God's hands by praying and trusting God to watch over them. Yes, at times, their decisions cause stress, but if the door of communication is wide open, they are much more likely to come to you before making a crucial decision because they can rely on you for advice given with love and compassion. Use these opportunities to teach your teen by demonstrating self-control and patience.

#3: Work Ethic and Serving

Most parents are content if they can get their teens to contribute around the house with at least one chore. Some parents pay their kids to do chores or only pay for extra chores outside the required ones. Every parent decides how they prefer to do it, but their work should be recognized and encouraged. If not at a younger age, then certainly by their teen years, children need to start learning to work and contribute to the household. The attitude toward work should be doing our work as if we are working for God and not for people. This concept differs from the common idea of working for themselves or others, as in volunteering. However, it makes sense when you think about how much better the quality of work might be when you are doing it for God. The outcome of your work should then be your very best every time and not careless or subpar.

Getting out there and volunteering with your teen is also an excellent idea. Some parents' response to this might be, "What? I can barely get my kid to do a chore. Getting him to volunteer would be like pulling teeth!" Well, it's worth a try. Serving helps them grow spiritually and build their faith. An overseas mission trip is almost life-changing, but only some parents can afford the time or money to arrange a mission trip. There are always opportunities to serve through your church or local charities. A mother adamant about getting her son to volunteer had a good idea. Her son was determined to work toward applying for entry into his favorite university. She told him that listing volunteer work on his college application would help. She was already a volunteer as a small group leader for the church youth group, so she found a volunteer opening for her son there to set up games each week for the youth group. He ended up enjoying it and making friends in the process and learned that volunteering brings the satisfaction of serving God with his time.

#4: Praying

There is a spiritual realm. It is good and evil, as mentioned at the beginning of this book. Satan has been in the world since the fall of Adam and Eve. However, God's children have authority over this enemy. Not everything will play out as expected when your family serves God. Trials will come, and the enemy attacks because he knows his time is short, as the return of Jesus for His children is soon. When facing brutal spiritual attacks, pray for deliverance. There are a couple of instances in the Bible where a child is brought to Jesus for deliverance from spiritual oppression. In Luke 9 of the Bible, there is an account of a man who begs Jesus to cast out an evil spirit that caused his son to scream and have convulsions. Jesus did rebuke the unclean spirit and healed the boy. And He gives us the power to do this today. Don't be afraid if your child faces danger or is overcome by temptation or addiction. It is a spiritual attack, and God has given you and your child the authority to pray and command the evil spirits away, as Jesus showed us.

According to Mark 16:17, believers have God-given authority to defend themselves from evil forces. Those who are committed to following Jesus have God's Holy Spirit in them and can practice prayer for deliverance. Teach your child that God's power works in us and through us so they can pray with confidence with authority from God. He promises us that His grace is sufficient for us and that His power is perfected in weakness.

#5 The Armor of God

Pray for your teen to put on the armor of God. Because there is a spiritual realm and we strive to remain in the spirit of God, the enemy is also at work, often trying to distract and destroy God's children and their families. The Bible warns us to be ready for the devil's evil plans by putting on the armor of God, which is described fully in Ephesians 6:

"Therefore, take up the full armor of God so that you will be able to resist on the evil day, and having done everything, to stand firm. Stand firm therefore, having belted your waist with truth, and having put on the breastplate of righteousness, and having strapped on your feet the preparation of the gospel of peace; in addition to all, taking up the shield of faith with which you will be able to extinguish all the flaming arrows of the evil one. And take the helmet of salvation and the sword of the Spirit, which is the Word of God." (New American Standard Version Bible, 2020, Eph. 6:11–17)

The armor of God describes attributes that the Lord will give His people to protect their minds and hearts. The first of the tools is the belt of truth, which is Jesus, God's true Word. The second tool is the breastplate of righteousness, which protects the heart from sin. The shoes of peace refer to going out and sharing the good news of salvation that Jesus gives. The shield of faith gives us God's protection against fiery arrows of evil attacks. The helmet of salvation protects the head (mind) against doubt from the enemy. The sword of the Spirit refers to God's Word, which is the Bible. Having God's Word in your heart and quoting scriptures fends off evil spiritual attacks.

Modeling good habits and virtuous character for your teen is the seventh step toward a better parent-teen relationship. Striving to live a life for God with these virtuous attributes is not easy. In fact, it gets more difficult in this increasingly anti-Christian culture. However, it is now essential more than ever to live out virtues since the Bible says, "Now for this very reason also, applying all diligence, in your faith supply moral excellence, and in your moral excellence, knowledge, and in your knowledge, self-control, and in your self-control, perseverance, and in your perseverance, godliness." (New American Standard Version Bible, 2020, 2 Peter 1:5-7). Remember that your teen is watching you and will likely follow in your footsteps. This is one reason to keep doing difficult things and making the right choices. The reward is God blessing you, your teen, and your entire family.

8

Conclusion

What a journey! Congratulations on your effort to parent your teen through faith. Let's review the seven steps to an improved parent-teen relationship.

1. Seek God for healing and reconcile broken relationships, first with God, and then with your teen. Work on providing one-on-one time with your teen, and ensure they have a maternal and paternal influence. Reconcile with empathy, listening, and humility. With God on your side, you can become more influential than outsiders to your teen and guide them with God's standards and wisdom provided in the Bible, the real truth. You can begin fostering good behavior in your child by modeling it yourself first. You can begin building stronger family relationships with God in the center.

2. Know who your true adversary is. Avoid the deception that God is not on your side because it is quite the opposite. Even those who choose to follow and seek God will face trials, but God is pursuing you and wants to bless all areas of your relationships, especially with your family. Don't let the enemy distort your perception and steal that from you. God is the One who can carry and guide you through the challenging phases of parenting. Establish God's Word as your home's ultimate authority, absolute truth, and moral standard. Teach your child clear standards and boundaries, and don't bail them out of consequences all the time. Guide them with love from childlike tantrums to more mature ways of thinking. When your child sees you love and accept them but will not tolerate their mischief, they will be much more inclined to be receptive to your guidance.

3. Recognize technology as one of the three most significant channels of intrusion that collide with parenting efforts and your teen's spiritual growth. When not

examined and managed carefully, it can weaken their faith and lead to a distorted worldview and self-perception. You now know that the enemy can impact a child's impressionable mind. He can do so through inappropriate, explicit, or abusive social media content and messages. Alternatively, your child might gain access to occult games that can trigger anger and existing violent tendencies, causing children to spiral out of control. When addicted to digital content, children can suffer and harm themselves and others, even the people they love. You know to monitor and become familiar with that content and teach your child to be a critical consumer using it responsibly, to use it intentionally in a way that honors God.

4. Be aware of the intrusion in media and culture. Music and movies tend to dominate teenagers' fields of interest. The cultural products allowed today would likely have been unheard of only a decade ago. However, the limits are shifting further and further toward more liberal philosophies that pose little to no boundaries for what will be considered appropriate for children of different ages. As a parent, you can now intentionally help them guard their heart and mind against it by having conversations about it with your child.

5. Take a look at your child's education with the understanding that it is a major contributor to your child's development of moral reasoning, habits and worldview. Schools that should teach valuable knowledge often promote political causes and ideologies that don't serve an educational purpose. You, as parents, have the right to protect and advocate for your child against these influences. You are also now aware of the benefits of alternatives to public education that may be more conducive to your child's learning and growth mentally and spiritually.

6. Recognize your child's needs in terms of mind, body, and spirit, focusing on the importance of physical and spiritual health. Keep peace in the home with established parental authority, grace, forgiveness, listening, self-control, prayers, and Bible reading. Assure them they are valued and important and that Jesus loves them and died for them. Have patience as you work toward bringing them to faith through prayer and repentance of sin, establishing their identity in Christ. They can practice their faith in daily tasks and get involved at church and within your community. A happy and healthy family starts with you.

Sleep quality directly affects your mental and physical health. Trust that God will protect you from any adverse outcomes, and don't punish yourself by denying yourself the gift of health. Eat well, sleep well, address your marital or relationship problems, and build a strong foundation for your child to lean on. Ultimately, when you are physically well and your love for God is solid, it spills over to your relationship with your teen and others. God is your strength in your weakness.

7. Focus on building biblical character and virtues with your children, such as a biblical view of money, work ethic, gratitude, and compassion. Help them develop healthy discipline, never in anger. Lastly, spiritual oppression needs a door. Those doors open when people are in distress and suffering. Oppression happens when adults and children attempt to resolve problems or fill a void with various forms of indulgence and modern spiritualism. Educate your teen, take a stance against these destructive influences, and teach them to guard their hearts and minds against negative spiritual attacks by putting on the full armor of God and saying prayers of deliverance.

Don't carry burdens alone. Seek support and help from God-fearing friends, professional faith-based counselors, and pastors for yourself and your teen. Even if you do not see results immediately, your teens listen and ponder your words and actions. Keep planting the seeds of faith. In God's time, hopefully soon, you will see the fruit!

One question for you: Don't you want your children to have friends and co-workers who also have Godly faith when they are grown? Then we should care not just about our own children but the children in other families, in other schools, on the other side of town, and on the other side of the world! Don't hide the Light. The world seems to be getting darker and more difficult for our children but all this means is that the Light shines brighter – through us. Thank you in advance for submitting a review and praying. God will do the rest. Leaving an honest review of this book will help other readers find this book and ultimately, the guidance from God they need for their relationship with their teen.

The next book ***Inspirational 30-Day Affirmation Challenge for Teens: Boost Your Mood, Fuel Your Faith & Be Inspired*** has been included with this book. It's a valuable tool to nurture faith in God with your teen in only about 5 minutes a day! If you would like to stay connected to Scriptseeds sign up for exclusive access to sneak peaks of upcoming books, giveaways, and faith boosting content at https://scriptseeds.com/connect. Begin to experience a faith transformation today!

Inspirational 30 Day Affirmation Challenge for Teens

Boost Your Mood, Fuel Your Faith & Be Inspired

by

Scriptseeds

INTRODUCTION

Congrats on stepping up to take the 30-day inspirational affirmation challenge! The fact that this book made it into your hands is not by chance. Whether you received it as a gift or picked it out of curiosity, God knows you have a need and wants to help you through this book.

Your first thought may be, "What the heck is an affirmation?" According to the American Heritage Dictionary, an affirmation is an act of affirming or the state of being affirmed; assertion. Well, duh, that doesn't help. Okay, so what does affirm mean? Again, according to the American Heritage dictionary, it means to declare positively and assert to be true. So basically, you'll be stating things positively to be true.

This is necessary because there is so much power in stating something and pondering it, whether it be solely about yourself or your relationship with others and the world around you. Have you ever been around a friend who is a constant "Debbie downer" and always says depressing and negative things? Do you also observe that this friend does not appear happy or does not have many friends? It may be because no one wants to be around someone who makes them feel bummed out and bored. No one wants to invite a Debbie downer to a party because they will just ruin good vibes. On the other hand, a friend who is usually happy and has an upbeat outlook on life is a lot more fun to be around, more attractive and even influential. That's what you want.

The only problem is some days or even today, you may have some drama or troubles that bring you so down that you don't even feel like smiling or talking to anyone. You just feel like chillin by yourself and listening to your music which sometimes just makes you feel worse, like if you're having a pity party.

That's where this challenge comes into play. Taking 5 minutes a day to read one affirmation and reflect on it throughout the day can get you through a crappy, difficult day all because you have a different mindset that started with an inspirational thought at the start of the day.

The best part of taking this challenge is that you invite God into your life by reading scriptures supporting each affirmation. The reason each affirmation is supported by a Bible scripture is that the scriptures have a lot of power. The Bible says that "For the word of God is living and active, and sharper than any two-edged sword, even penetrating as far as the division of soul and spirit, of both joints and marrow, and able to judge the thoughts and intentions of the heart" (New American Standard Bible, 2020, Heb 4:12). The truth is life throws many unfair arrows at us especially when we're young and a have a lot of positive things going for us. The devil does not want us to succeed and wants to take away what God has given us: happiness, love, compassion, kindness, goodness and self-control.

If you think about it, it's like a real-life video game. The devil's role is to kill, steal and destroy, but your mission is to defeat him daily with the tools God gives you, the most powerful tool being his Word which is the Bible scriptures. And the more scriptures you rack up in your collection, the better you position yourself to win! Therefore reading an affirmation and scripture a day keeps the devil away! This is God's prescription for you to defeat the enemy and live your best life possible, an abundant life!

So let's get to it!

God will meet you where you are in order to take you where He wants you to go. – Tony Evans

I dedicate this book to my Lord Jesus Christ.

Dear Jesus, thank you for the teen who is holding this book in their hands today. Please let this book plant a seed in their heart and life that will grow and blossom into a forever relationship with you. Let them be open and receptive to your love and the awesome blessings you have in store for them. Empower this teen to put on the full armor of God and stand against the devil's schemes and have the boldness to be a light in the darkness. In Jesus' name Amen

Day 1

I can do what seems impossible

because Jesus has my back.

"I can do all things through Him who strengthens me" (New American Standard Version Bible, 2020, Phil. 4:13). If you have something coming up today that makes you have these dang butterflies in your stomach or makes you want to puke, like a speech assignment in class, a test or the first game of the season, just say this scripture and affirmation to yourself. Throughout the Bible, God selected the meekest and smallest people to do the most amazing, incredible things. So no matter how small you may feel, God gives you the authority and power to accomplish the task and do it like a champ. Even when you don't believe in yourself or God, He definitely believes in you!

You got this!

Day 2

I am unique, and I thank God

for making me this way.

"I will give thanks to You because I am awesomely and wonderfully made; wonderful are Your works, and my soul knows it very well" (New American Standard Version Bible, 2020, Ps. 139:14). Did you know almost everyone has a flaw they hate about themselves that no one else notices? If it is noticeable, they easily look past it because of the other attractive features that surround it. If you hate your nose or the gap between your teeth, it's likely the one thing someone out there secretly loves about you. If you change it, you change what makes you uniquely you. You also have unique characteristics and gifts or talents that God gave you and that even attract others to you. For example, a few celebrities out there didn't let their unusual physical traits set them back from their unique potential, like supermodel Winnie Harlow. She has a skin condition called vitiligo, a skin pigmentation issue where parts of her skin are lighter than others. But obviously, she knows she is still beautiful and continues to do what she does best. Who knows? Maybe she wouldn't be recognized or have the same impact in the modeling world if she changed her look. Other famous people who embraced their uniqueness are Kate Bosworth, with eyes of a different color, and the singer Seal, whose facial scarring came from an autoimmune condition. God knows every outer and inner part of you: the number of hairs on your head and every thought and emotion you have. He made you wonderfully and with the ability to do great things despite your physical features and worrisome thoughts. The whole chapter of Psalm 139 talks about this, and it is a super cool chapter to read when you feel self-critical.

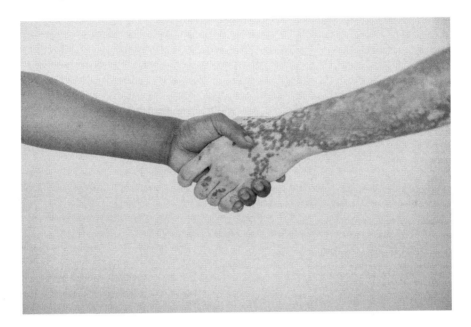

Day 3

God gives me peace

and guards my heart and my mind.

"And the peace of God, which surpasses all comprehension, will guard your hearts and your minds in Christ Jesus" (New American Standard Version Bible, 2020, Phil. 4:7)

Have you ever experienced a time when you should be worried or upset about something bad that happened, but you weren't and instead were calm? Well, it's because you had peace about it. When we have our hearts and minds focused on God and what He has given us and done for us, we have faith and peace that everything will work itself out. Sometimes just saying a prayer and talking to God as if he is your friend gives you this peace that drowns out the anxiety you would otherwise have. An example would be when a jerk keeps harassing you or trying to put you down, and you can easily blow it off because either you know what they're saying is not true, or even if it is true, it's not something that you will let get in your way of being awesome. Extraordinary people who get knocked down always get back up again and become stronger. If you let it get to you, the bully wins, and so does the devil, but if you keep your chin up, and walk off with authority in Jesus, then you win because he failed to trigger a response from you like he wanted to. Even though he may be laughing, it's a front. He really feels dumb and runs off with his tail between his legs! If they get physically aggressive, it's not cool and has to be reported to authorities as an assault. Let someone know so it will stop.

Day 4

I am not afraid because God is with me.

"Have I not commanded you? Be strong and courageous. Do not be terrified or dismayed, for the Lord your God is with you wherever you go." (New American Standard Version Bible, 2020, Josh. 1:9). Joshua, a military leader, had to do something nerve-wracking that God asked him to do: cross a big river and take over a land that God promised them. He had to get help from the officers and lead them, but he did it! If you are faced with doing something today that seems impossible, don't listen to negative thoughts in your head like, "I'm not ready", or "I'm not good enough". Take the lead or take the first step and be brave, even if you need to ask for a bit of help, and the rest will get easier. You can do it because God is with you!

Day 5

I am confident in what I say.

Think before you speak is a piece of advice commonly taught. Many teachers turn the word THINK into an acronym for the following questions:

Is it **T**rue?

Is it **H**elpful?

Is it **I**nspiring?

Is it **N**ecessary?

Is it **K**ind?

While this is a cool acronym, knowing how God feels about what we say is more important. "May the words of my mouth and the mediation of my heart be acceptable in Your sight, Lord, my rock and my Redeemer" (New American Standard Version Bible, 2020, Ps. 19:14). So today, try pausing before you say something and ask yourself "Would it be acceptable to God for me to say it?" If so, say it! If you practice this, you should find that you are cutting back on unintentionally saying hurtful or unkind words, gossiping and things that even hurt yourself because the more you say or repeat something, even in your mind or to yourself, the more you start to believe it.

Instead, be one of those people who say things that uplift, encourage and help someone. Everyone wants to be around someone who spreads joy and hope!

Day 6

God gives me wisdom and directs my path.

If you find yourself in a situation where something doesn't seem right and you're hesitant, that's God convicting you or nudging you. It may be because it isn't right. This would be the time to seek God's wisdom and input. Look up what the Bible says about a circumstance using a Bible concordance. Talk to your parents or a pastor who can help you through a tough decision. That's why God put these people in your life. A Proverb in the Bible says, "Trust in the Lord with all your heart and do not lean on your own understanding. In all your ways acknowledge Him and He will make your paths straight." (New American Standard Version Bible, 2020, Prov 3:5-6). And don't worry if you make a mistake. It's not too late to seek God and redirect yourself toward God's path or apologize to someone negatively affected. His mercies are new every morning!

On the other hand, be careful when someone gives you bad advice. The Bible instructs, "Beloved, do not believe every spirit, but test the spirits to see whether they are from God, because many false prophets have gone out into the world." (New American Standard Version Bible, 2020, 1 John 4:1). Yep, there are haters out there that hate so much they intentionally want to trip you up. So if it doesn't align with what the Bible says, then look the other way and go to God.

Day 7

I am not a slave to sin. I am free!

Most people only think of drug addicts or alcoholics as being stuck in their sin or a slave to it but this applies to all of us at some point. The Bible says in the book of Romans, "For all have sinned and fall short of the glory of God" (New American Standard Version Bible, 2020, Rom. 3:23). So if we have not repented of our sin, any sin, we are still slaves to sin. Romans 6:16 says, "Do you not know that the one to whom you present yourselves as slaves for obedience, you are slaves of that same one whom you obey, either of sin, resulting in death, or of obedience, resulting in righteousness?" Being a slave to sin is NOT freedom. It is fun for a little bit but ultimately will lead to a dead end and some damage or loss, so it's not worth it. Another scripture that illustrates this is gross and makes you wonder why you love your dog so much. A Proverb in the Bible says, "Like a dog that returns to his vomit, so is a fool who repeats his foolishness" (New American Standard Version Bible, 2020, Prov. 26:11). Why would anyone want to continue sin if it's just toxic and bad? We are just as bad as this dog, and this is where we need intervention. We cannot rid ourselves of sin on our own. Jesus sets us free as it says in John 8:36, "So if the Son sets you free, you will be free indeed!"

DAY 8

Even though I failed, I am forgiven!

In addition to the Ten Commandments, there were so many other laws in the Bible. There are many Bible rules about what not to eat, how to do things fairly regarding possessions and property, handling money, and more. But it's not that God wants to be strict with us. On the contrary, he wants to protect us from harm. He knew that if people lived by them, they would live in harmony and avoid disease, drama and sin, which separates us from God. But he also knew that people would not be able to keep up with them all because we're sinful by nature, so people had to sacrifice animals in the Old Testament to cover for those areas of sin where they fell short. "And almost all things are cleansed with blood, according to the Law, and without the shedding of blood there is no forgiveness." (New American Standard Version Bible, 2020, Heb. 9:22). The Ten Commandments show how Holy God is and how we are not. We can never meet His standards on our own, so the consequence of breaking God's law is death and hell. So God sent His Son Jesus to die on the cross for us, as it says in John 3:16. The way Ray Comfort of Living Waters explains it, just like in a court of law where we broke the moral law (The Ten Commandments) we should be judged and sentenced, but Jesus came and paid the fine letting us go free! Romans 5:8 says, "But God demonstrates His own love toward us, in that while we were still sinners, Christ died for us" (New American Standard Version Bible, 2020, Rom. 5:8). This bridges that huge gap between God and us.

Here is a challenge within this 30-day challenge. The challenge is to give God a chance to show Himself to you. Let Him show you how He can make a difference in your life permanently, well beyond just 30 days and even into eternity if you repent and just trust in Him just like you would trust a parachute to save you when jumping from an airplane, as Ray says. The Bible says, "That if you confess with your mouth Jesus as Lord, and believe in your heart that God raised Him from the dead, you will be saved." (New American Standard Version Bible, 2020, Rom. 10:9)

Trust God with your life. Turn away from your bad habits and sins. Give thanks to God for sending Jesus to die on the cross to save you from your sins. He will help you live a life that honors Him.

Day 9

I am a light in the darkness.

If you have come this far in the challenge and have decided to live your life committed to following God, congrats! You have passed from death and darkness to light; therefore, you have the light from God that you can share with others. There is so much darkness and suffering in the world that comes in many forms and many have lost hope and have no one to turn to. If someone like that crosses your path today, take the time to be a light in their darkness. If a friend of yours is unhappy or even rude, it could be because they are having problems that no one knows about or understands. You could be the one person who makes their day. It could simply be a smile, listening with compassion, a helping hand or just making them laugh. "You are the light of the world. A city set on a hill cannot be hidden. Nor do people light a lamp, and put it under the basket, but on the lampstand; and it gives light to all who are in the house. (New American Standard Version Bible, 2020, Matt. 5:14-15) Sharing some of these affirmations and scriptures with a hurting friend can help defeat the enemy's attacks in their life too.

Day 10

I'm grateful for God's creation.

Take the time to get out in nature or step outside tonight and look at the moon. Did you know that the moon's cycle is used as the marker for time? It takes about a month for the moon to orbit the earth! God created the moon and stars not just to provide light at night and time but also to mark signs and seasons! The most amazing thing is that two people hundreds of miles from each other can see the moon simultaneously as it stands suspended in the night sky. And God said, "'Let there be lights in the expanse of the heavens to separate the day from the night. and they shall serve as signs and for seasons and days and years." (New American Standard Version Bible, 2020, Gen. 1:14)

DAY 11

Whenever I do work, I will do my best for God.

If you have a task ahead of you today, strive to put in extra effort and see how you feel after completing it. If you have a school assignment, study and read more than you usually do. If it's a chore, do it better than before, or do an extra chore without being asked. If you have a job after school, do it as if God is your boss. Colossians 3:17 says "Whatever you do in word or deed, do everything in the name of the Lord Jesus, giving thanks to God the Father." (New American Standard Version Bible, 2020, Col. 3:17) You will not only feel better about your accomplishment but you will please God.

Day 12

I can set a goal and reach it.

Do you have a dream or a picture of what you want your life to look like someday? If it is something that would honor God and at the same time bring you happiness, then you should definitely work toward it! Start by praying about it because although God knows what we want, He still wants us to come to him like a child asks his father. Set short-term goals and long-term goals. Work toward the short-term ones with reasonable dates, so it's not overwhelming. As long as you have faith, commitment, and work hard with perseverance, you can certainly achieve it. 2 Chronicles 15:7 says, "But you, be strong and do not lose courage for there is a reward for your work." (New American Standard Version Bible, 2020, 2 Chron. 15:7)

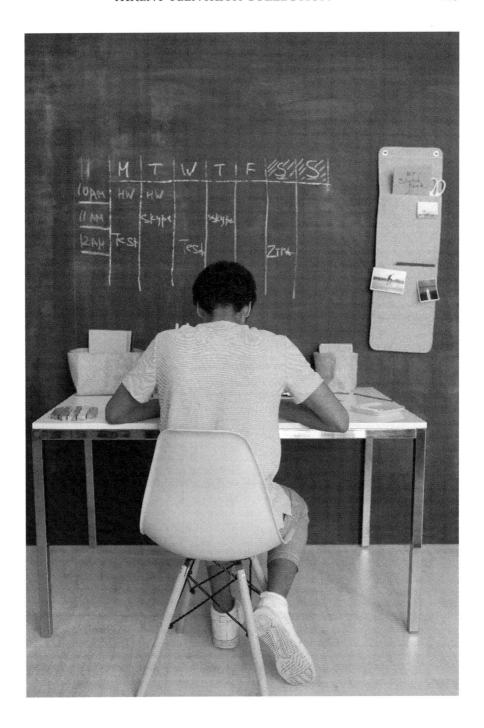

DAY 13

I'm thankful for a new day.

God gives us a new day every day. It's always a chance to start over and make the best of the time throughout that day. It's up to you to decide how to spend this precious time God gave you today. "This is the day which the Lord has made; Let's rejoice and be glad in it." (New American Standard Version Bible, 2020, Ps. 118:24). Do something good that will make today memorable, like doing something with a sibling. Make something artistic, ride a bike or do something that does not involve the internet. Offline activities and time away from screens seem to make time slow down a little bit so you can enjoy being a teen. One day you just might miss it.

DAY 14

I have everything I need because God provides.

There are many names for God listed throughout the Bible. One of them is Jehovah-Jireh which means God will provide. Just as your parents provide your basic needs, God provides all of our needs because He loves us. "Consider the ravens, that they neither sow nor reap; they have no storeroom nor barn; and yet God feeds them: how much more valuable you are than the birds!" (New American Standard Version Bible, 2020, Luke 12:24) So don't worry. God will provide what you need and even what you want at the right time - His time.

Day 15

I am loved.

What is one way to extend your lifespan? By honoring your parents! Just as God sets rules out because he loves us, parents, grandparents, and other guardians also set rules for your safety and to teach you certain principles for life because they love you and care for you. "Honor your father and mother (which is the first commandment with a promise), so that it may turn out well for you, and that you may live long on the earth. (New American Standard Version Bible, 2020, Eph. 6:2-3) Parents, grandparents, or guardians are not perfect, and God is always working on them just as He is working on you. But remember, they are doing their best to raise you and set you up for success. So give them respect, love them back, and give them grace when they seem annoying to you. Sometimes it's tough love, but that's better love than if they just let you do whatever you want to do. Many teens out there don't have that and wish they did.

Day 16

God blesses me with a good friend.

Some people are very outgoing or extroverted, and others are introverted. Whether you have one or many friends, today is a good day to start looking at your friends. Who are they, really? Take a deep look at them by observing what they say, their worldview, and how they treat others. Are you proud of who they are? The Bible says, "Do not be deceived: Bad company corrupts good morals." (New American Standard Version Bible, 2020, 1 Cor. 15:33). If you don't want to be associated with the characteristics your friends have, then gently and slowly distance yourself a little and ask God to bring other like-minded friends into your life. Surround yourself with friends who have the same worldview as you. Find friends with characteristics you eventually want for yourself because they are less likely to pull along a destructive path and instead build you up.

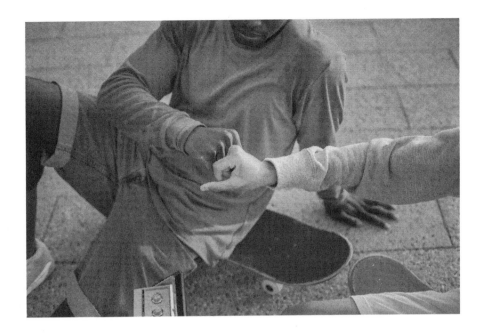

Day 17

I appreciate the body God gave me. I am gorgeous.

Someday you may see someone of the opposite sex and say to yourself, "Clearly, there is a God." or "Thank God for His Creation!" Someone at some point will feel that way about you and your body. Your body is sacred as the Bible says, "Or do you not know that your body is the temple of the Holy Spirit within you, whom you have from God and that you are not your own? For you have been bought for a price: therefore glorify God in your body." (New American Standard Version Bible, 2020, 1 Cor. 6:19-20). This means that we belong to God because we acknowledge that Jesus paid the price for our sins. We are His and cannot just give ourselves over to sin. Even a boyfriend or girlfriend needs to respect your standards. Having your body is not their privilege. It's only a spouse's privilege. So it's best to avoid putting ourselves in a situation where we will be tempted to sin. Instead, we should take care of our bodies by staying sexually pure, taking care of our appearance, eating healthy food and exercising. That's what God wants for you.

Day 18

I am a giving person.

God is so generous with us. He gives us a beautiful earth with everything we need in it. He provides us with capable bodies so that we can play and work. So we should also be generous with our time and money to others in need. Galatians 6:2 says, "Bear one another's burdens and thereby fulfill the law of Christ." (New American Standard Version Bible, 2020, Gal. 6:2) Ask God for an opportunity to give today. After all, everything we have comes from God, so we should cheerfully give back.

Day 19

I will prosper and have success.

There are no guarantees in life. Only God sees the big picture and knows our future. But there is a high probability that because you have a relationship with Jesus and you follow Him, you have a pretty good chance that you will prosper and succeed. In the book of Joshua, it is written, "This Book of the Law shall not depart from your mouth, but you shall meditate on it day and night, so that you may be careful to do according to all that is written in it; for then you will make your way prosperous, and then you will achieve success." (New American Standard Version Bible, 2020, Josh. 1:8) If you strive to do the next right thing and ask God for guidance in everything you do, you'll be on the right track.

Day 20

I am confident.

If you feel you are not good enough because you are comparing yourself to others, remember you are not like everyone else. You are unique in that you may learn differently, think differently, and act differently because of your personality and God-given gifts and talents. If everyone were the same, this world would be boring. But because you and your friends or siblings have various personalities, you can complement each other and make a good team when you put your strengths together. Jeremiah 17:7 says, "Blessed is the man who trusts in the Lord, and whose trust is in the Lord." (New American Standard Version Bible, 2020, Jer. 17:7). So don't stress. You are the best! And you are enough. Don't worry about impressing others. God knows your heart and that you're being honest and being your best. Put the rest in God's hands, and he will give you strength in your weakness.

Day 21

My labor is not in vain.

What are the motives behind your goals? Is the point of your end goal to serve God or yourself? When you work toward your goals to serve God, God will bless your work. "Therefore, my beloved brothers and sisters, be firm, immovable, always excelling in the work of the Lord, knowing that your labor is not vain in the Lord." (New American Standard Version Bible, 2020, 1 Cor. 15:58). You don't have to be a missionary, pastor or Sunday School teacher to serve God. If you want to, then great! But there are so many opportunities in every industry to make an impact for God. Ask God to show you what His path is for you so you can start surrounding yourself with those types of jobs or people and preparing yourself for that type of work by asking lots of questions. Then you will be an awesome servant of God!

Day 22

I can do difficult things.

"Consider it all joy, my brothers and sisters, when you encounter various trials, knowing that the testing of your faith produces endurance. And let endurance have its perfect result, so that you may be perfect and complete, lacking in nothing." (New American Standard Version Bible, 2020, James 1:2-4) Are you facing any difficult trail? You're probably wondering, "How the heck can I find joy in a trial?" Well, you can look forward to a great outcome that you're hoping to see at the end when it's all over, even if it's hard to visualize it now. That's having faith. You can also see that there may be other things that have worked out in your favor and that the situation could've been a lot worse or way more difficult than it really is. And you could see this as a test of your faith! You can look back at this difficult trial someday and say, "Wow, how in the world did God get me through that? I don't know, but He did! And something good came out of it!"

Day 23

I have hope.

Something may seem impossible or not exactly going your way right now. Maybe you're tired and feel like giving up already. If you were someone who did not have a relationship with God, it would be very easy to lose hope and you may have a good reason to give up. However, you DO know God and the promises in the Bible. A promise in the Bible says, "For I know the plans that I have for you, declares the Lord, plans for prosperity and not for disaster, to give you a future and a hope." (New American Standard Version Bible, 2020, Jer. 29:11) So now is not the time to give up! If it's school you are struggling with, keep studying, be diligent and it will get easier. If it's a job you're struggling with, keep working at it and put in 100% so you can move on to something bigger and better more quickly. If it's a personal or relationship issue, pray about it as often as possible. You can't go wrong. It will pay off and God will bless you a ton.

Day 24

I am strong.

Today you may be trying to stand your ground against someone or something negative. Remember you have God on your side and He is your strength. "Yet those who wait for the Lord will gain new strength. They will mount up with wings like eagles; they will run and not get tired; they will walk and not become weary." (New American Standard Version Bible, 2020, Isa. 40:31) Pray for God to show you how to respond to that negativity. Put it in God's hands, meaning don't stress and try to figure it all out yourself. Just know that God will defend you and keep you safe. Talking to loved ones you trust will also help you feel at ease and relieve some anxiety. Thank God for parents, pastors and good friends!

Day 25

I am teachable.

According to a Forbes article, being humble and teachable leads one to success. It shows that you appreciate the knowledge of a teacher, parent, or coach trying to impart knowledge. Be receptive and make the most of it as you apply it. Be a good listener and take action on any suggestions or corrections they advise. "All Scripture is God-breathed and useful for teaching, rebuking, correcting and training in righteousness." (New American Standard Version Bible, 2020, 2 Tim. 3:16-17) More importantly, God wants to teach you through his Word, the Bible. So if you discover that some habit you have or the way you do something is not aligned with God's Word, then correct it and follow God's teaching. A beautiful future is waiting for you if you can practice these attributes.

Day 26

I am safe.

If you are living in fear, remember that God is your protector. A good scripture to read or memorize to recall when you are afraid is "I will say to the Lord, "My refuge and my fortress, my God, in whom I trust!". (New American Standard Version Bible, 2020, Ps. 91:2). Fear is from the enemy and having fear for a long time is unhealthy. Pray for God to give you peace and comfort. If you can find someone to confide in about your fear and pray with you, that's also very comforting. God does not want you to be in fear and sometimes provides us comfort through others, so don't be afraid to share it with someone you trust, like a parent or relative.

Day 27

God comforts me.

There are sad parts of life that can't be avoided, like death. If you lose someone close, you might miss this person sometimes, especially when certain things may remind you of them. Maybe someone close to you has to move far away and you worry that you may never see this person again. Other tragedies happen, like when parents divorce, losing your home or your dear pet you loved so much. Jesus said, "Blessed are those who mourn, for they will be comforted." (New American Standard Version Bible, 2020, Matt. 5:4) God has compassion and sees your tears. It's okay to cry and let God comfort you. In time, you will be healed and God will restore joy and peace in your heart. During times like these, you need God the most, so stay close to Him and He will pull you through this difficult time.

Day 28

God cares about my desires.

Don't ever fall for the lie that God is too busy for you or is not concerned with small things that are important to you. He knows and cares about every desire you have. When you genuinely worship God and follow His ways in every way you can, God will fulfill your desires. A promise in the Bible to hold on to is "Take delight in the Lord and He will give you the desires of your heart." (New American Standard Version Bible, 2020, Ps. 37:4) What is your desire? Talk to God about it in prayer!

Day 29

I am not alone.

Unexpected things may happen, things that didn't turn out the way you thought they would. Sometimes this can be scary because the outcome is still unknown and you worry so much that you can't sleep or stop thinking about it. God does not want you to worry. Worrying excessively means you're not having faith in your heavenly Father. Remember, the Bible says, "Be strong and courageous, do not be afraid or in dread of them, for the Lord your God is the One who is going with you. He will not desert you or abandon you." (New American Standard Version Bible, 2020, Deut. 31:6) He loves you!

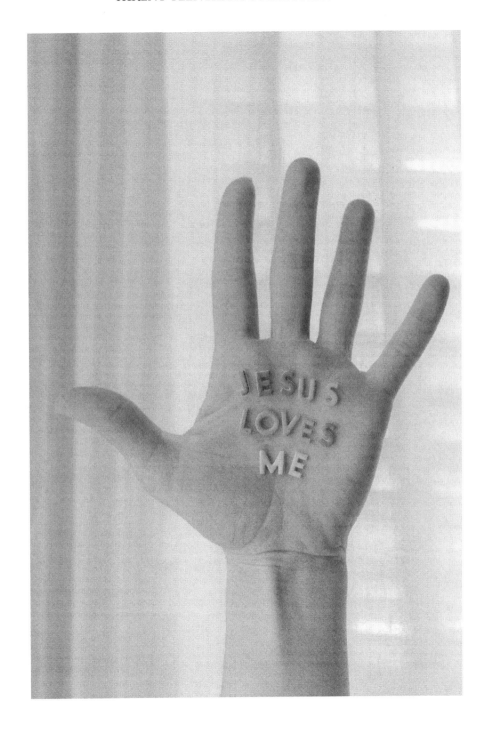

Day 30

God speaks to me when I'm quiet.

God may not speak audibly to you, but when you listen more and talk less, you will not only learn a lot more by observations, but you may notice the subtle ways God speaks. "Even a fool, when he keeps silent, is considered wise; when he closes his lips, he is considered prudent." (New American Standard Version Bible, 2020, Prov. 17:28) If you have ever tried talking and listening simultaneously, you will definitely miss what another person is saying. Sometimes God speaks to us through a person or multiple people. Sometimes God speaks to us internally when we pray and meditate on the scriptures. So being quiet and listening is a skill worth practicing. The more we do it, the more we will hear from God.

Conclusion

Great job! You should be stoked that you completed the 30-day inspirational affirmation challenge! Now you can take it a step further by diving deeper into the Bible, which nourishes your soul.

A vitamin is meant to supplement your diet with real food. We don't always get the vitamins we need from the meals we eat throughout the day, so we'll take vitamin C or iron to supplement, but would you be able to survive on just supplements every day and very little food? You might still be hungry because you're still missing protein, complex carbs, fiber and so on.

Reading an affirmation each day is like taking a vitamin. It's helpful on a small scale but even better to feed your soul more of God's Word. The Bible is God's gift to us. It is His love letter to us filled with true accounts that give us insight and understanding of how to live an abundant life. God wants us to live a happier, healthier life full of freedom through this instruction manual for life. A good place to start is in the book of John. It is the account of Jesus told by one of His disciples - John.

If you liked this Inspirational 30-Day Affirmation Challenge book, please leave a review. You can sign and date below that you completed the challenge and pass it on to another friend or keep it for yourself and do the challenge as many times as you like!

Challenge completed!

Name and Date: _____   _____

Use this space to write your thoughts and favorite scriptures.

RESOURCES BOOK 1

4 Ways To Outsmart Stress With Food - The Whole Journey. (n.d.). https://thewholejourney.com/blog/4-ways-to-outsmart-stress-with-food

Account, S. (2022, April 4). *God's Word Is True.* Focus on the Family. https://www.focusonthefamily.com/parenting/gods-word-is-true/

Adle, H. (2021, August 8). *Secular Music: Does it Have a Place in Christian Homes?* The Joyful Life Magazine. https://joyfullifemagazine.com/parenting-and-music/

ALEC SCHEMMEL, The National Desk. (2022, May 25). *State dept of education promotes "online chat spaces" for LGBT students as young as 10.* KATV. https://katv.com/news/nation-world/state-dept-of-education-promotes-online-chat-spaces-for-lgbt-students-as-young-as-10-arizona-qchat-gender-spectrum-questioning-trans-tensgender-gay-bisexual-lesbian

Alexander, C. (2022, July 11). *What is the TikTok blackout challenge? The dangerous trend that has parents suing.* Digital Trends. https://www.digitaltrends.com/mobile/what-is-tiktok-blackout-challenge-why-parents-suing/

American Academy of Child and Adolescent Psychiatry. (2017, September). *Teen Brain: Behavior, Problem Solving, and Decision Making.* Retrieved December 10, 2022, from https://www.aacap.org/AACAP/Families_and_Youth/Facts_for_Families/FFF-Guide/The-Teen-Brain-Behavior-Problem-Solving-and-Decision-Making-095.aspx

Are Scandinavian countries proof that Godless societies do better? (2021, January 8). [Video]. YouTube. Retrieved December 10, 2022, from https://www.youtube.com/watch?v=Plw1Az4M93s

Burgess, J. (2009, November 23). *Parenting: The Power of Words and Your Child*. Parenting Tips and Advice. Retrieved December 10, 2022, from https://www.more4kids.info/1581/parenting-and-the-power-of-words/

Burke, N. C. D. (2018a, April 13). *Is Your Child Getting Enough Vitamins and Minerals? A Guide to Testing for Nutritional Deficiencies (Part 1 – Vitamin D!) – Naturopathic Pediatrics*. https://naturopathicpediatrics.com/2018/04/13/child-getting-enough-vitamins-minerals-guide-testing-nutritional-deficiencies-part-1-vitamin-d/

Burke, N. C. D. (2018b, August 10). *Is Your Child Getting Enough Vitamins and Minerals? A Guide to Testing for Nutritional Deficiencies (Part 2 – B Vitamins!) – Naturopathic Pediatrics*. https://naturopathicpediatrics.com/2018/08/10/is-your-child-getting-enough-vitamins-and-minerals-a-guide-to-testing-for-nutritional-deficiencies-part-2-b-vitamins/

Burke, N. C. D. (2019, April 23). *Is Your Child Getting Enough Vitamins and Minerals? A Guide to Testing for Nutritional Deficiencies (Part 3 – Iron) – Naturopathic Pediatrics*. https://naturopathicpediatrics.com/2019/04/23/is-your-child-getting-enough-vitamins-and-minerals-a-guide-to-testing-for-nutritional-deficiencies-part-3-iron/

Carter, J. (2019, March 2). *How to Teach Children to Deal with Bullying*. The Gospel Coalition. https://www.thegospelcoalition.org/article/teach-children-deal-bullying/

Castelino, L. (2022, September 21). *Staying safe Online and on Social Media: An interview with Paul Davis*. Where Parents Talk. https://whereparentstalk.com/profiles-category/staying-safe-online-and-on-social-media-an-interview-with-paul-davis/

Center, N. S. C. &. F. G. (2021, May 6). *When Music Encourages Dangerous Behavior*. North Shore Child & Family Guidance Center. https://northshorechildguidance.org/when-music-encourages-dangerous-behavior/

CitizenLink & Focus on the Family Action. (2022). *Back To School For Parents*. Family Policy Alliance. Retrieved December 10, 2022, from https://familypolicyalliance.com/back-to-school-for-parents/?utm_source=newsletter

Clarke, J. (2022, August 17). *Speaking Life to Your Kids: Balancing Encouragement with Truth*. Intoxicated on Life. https://www.intoxicatedonlife.com/speaking-life-kids/

Clay, B. (2021, May 31). *Christian Education vs. Public School*. Answers in Genesis. https://answersingenesis.org/public-school/christian-education-vs-public-school/

Community, P. T. &. T. (2022, August 9). *The Unexpected But Genius Trick That Stopped Tech Battles With Our Teen*. parentingteensandtweens.com. https://parentingteensandtweens.com/the-unexpected-but-genius-trick-that-stopped-tech-battles-with-our-teen/

Demonic Doorways and Signs or Symptoms of Demonization/Demonic Oppression. (2022, December 5). Jesus Truth Deliverance. https://jesustruthdeliverance.com/demonic-doorways-and-signs-of-demonization/

Desk, L. (2022, June 10). *Teenager kills mother over PUBG: Experts on how online gaming can affect mental health*. The Indian Express. https://indianexpress.com/article/lifestyle/health/teenager-kills-mother-pubg-online-gaming-mental-health-7962375/

Dickson, E. (2021, March). *We Asked Satanists What They Think of the New Lil Nas X Video*. Rolling Stone. Retrieved December 10, 2022, from https://www.rollingstone.com/culture/culture-news/lil-nas-x-montero-call-me-by-your-name-video-church-of-satan-1147634/

Elliott, M. (2021, December 10). Understanding the 10 Commandments and their relevance for today. *Reporter-Times*. Retrieved December 11, 2022, from https://www.reporter-times.com/story/lifestyle/faith/2021/12/10/understanding-10-commandments-and-their-relevance-today/6457925001/

Engler, P. (2020, June 4). *3 Pros and Cons of Letting Your Family Listen to Secular Music*. Crosswalk.com.

https://www.crosswalk.com/family/parenting/pros-and-cons-of-letting-your-family-listen-to-secular-music.html

Foust, M. (2019, August 30). *8 Family-Friendly Alternatives to Netflix*. Crosswalk.com. https://www.crosswalk.com/culture/television/family-friendly-alternatives-to-netflix.html

Fowler, E. (2022, October 3). *Teach Kids to Serve God*. Child Evangelism Fellowship. https://www.cefonline.com/articles/teach-kids-articles/teach-kids-to-serve-god/

Giaimo, C. (2021, April 22). *How One of the World's Oldest Science Experiments Comes Up From the Dirt*. The New York Times. https://www.nytimes.com/2021/04/21/science/beal-seeds-experiment.html

Gilboa, D. (2020, September 11). *How to Counteract the Influence that Media Has on Teens*. Your Teen Magazine. https://yourteenmag.com/technology/influence-of-media-on-teenagers

GotQuestions.org. (2022a, January 4). *How is Satan god of this world (2 Corinthians 4:4)?* https://www.gotquestions.org/Satan-god-world.html

GotQuestions.org. (2022b, January 4). *What is the human condition according to the Bible?* https://www.gotquestions.org/human-condition.html

GotQuestions.org. (2022c, May 25). *Do human beings truly have a free will?* https://www.gotquestions.org/free-will.html

Hallowell, B. (2022, August 21). *Ex-psychic's WARNING after tarot cards, paranormal sparked 'rabbit hole of destruction.'* The Christian Post. https://www.christianpost.com/news/ex-psychics-warning-after-tarot-cards-lead-destruction.html

Haughee. (2014, September 29). Attachment Theory and the Gospel explored - God's Intent for relationships. *PACEs Connection*. Retrieved December 10, 2022, from https://www.pacesconnection.com/blog/attachment-theory-and-the-gospel-explored-god-s-intent-for-relationships

Holcomb, J., & Holcomb, L. (2021, October 8). *How to Help Children Who've Experienced Trauma.* The Gospel Coalition. https://www.thegospelcoalition.org/article/help-children-trauma/

How Dads Affect Their Daughters into Adulthood. (n.d.). Institute for Family Studies. https://ifstudies.org/blog/how-dads-affect-their-daughters-into-adulthood

How To Do Damage Control When You Fight In Front of Your Kids. (n.d.). https://www.ahaparenting.com/read/Do-You-Fight-In-Front-of-Your-Kids

How to handle stress in your children. (n.d.). Focus on the Family. https://www.focusonthefamily.ca/content/how-to-handle-stress-in-your-children

How to trust God with your older children. (2017, October 10). The Courage. https://www.thecourage.com/how-to-trust-god-with-your-older-children/

How Working Parents Can Prioritize Sleep. (2021, August 30). Harvard Business Review. https://hbr.org/2020/03/how-working-parents-can-prioritize-sleep

Hubbard, G. (2021, June 1). *Ep. 019 | The Dangers of Scolding.* GingerHubbard. https://www.gingerhubbard.com/blogs/gingers-blog/ep-019-the-dangers-of-scolding

Is Reality TV Influencing Teens to Get Plastic Surgery? | About Plastic Surgery. (n.d.). https://www.aboutplasticsurgery.com/is-reality-tv-influencing-teens-to-get-plastic-surgery/

Is The Bible Reliable?—Seven Questions | Bible.org. (n.d.). https://bible.org/article/bible-reliable%E2%80%94seven-questions

Jackson, T., Koushank, A., & Tengergen, G. (2022). *Challenges and Solutions to Implementing a Community-Based Wellness Program for Non-Offending Minor Attracted Persons.* Journal of Child Sexual Abuse. Retrieved December 10, 2022, from https://www.tandfonline.com/doi/full/10.1080/10538712.2022.2056103

Jiang, J. (2020, August 14). *How Teens and Parents Navigate Screen Time and Device Distractions.* Pew Research Center: Internet, Science & Tech. Retrieved December 11, 2022, from https://www.pewresearch.org/internet/2018/08/22/how-teens-and-parents-navigate-screen-time-and-device-distractions/

John Weisâs review of Recovering the Lost Tools of Learning. (n.d.). https://www.goodreads.com/review/show/1145354961

Johnson, A. (2021, November 19). *Kenneth Copeland - Your Thoughts Are Connected to Your Physical Body Â».* Online Sermons 2022. Retrieved December 10, 2022, from https://online-sermons.org/kennethcopeland/1874-kenneth-copeland-your-thoughts-are-connected-to-your-physical-body.html

Kaliszewsk, M., PhD. (2022, September 15). *The Entertainment Industry and Addiction in America.* American Addiction Centers. Retrieved December 10, 2022, from https://americanaddictioncenters.org/blog/entertainments-influence-on-addiction

Krumbeck, E. (2022, April 7). *Nutritional interventions for depression and anxiety in children – Naturopathic Pediatrics.* https://naturopathicpediatrics.com/2022/04/07/nutritional-interventions-food-depression-and-anxiety-children-pediatrics/

Levine, A. S. (2022, April 27). *How TikTok Live Became 'A Strip Club Filled With 15-Year-Olds.'* Forbes. https://www.forbes.com/sites/alexandralevine/2022/04/27/how-tiktok-live-became-a-strip-club-filled-with-15-year-olds/?sh=3e3d475962d7

Lewolt, L. (2021, May 19). *MISPLACED - Overcoming Depression and Healing From the Heartbreaks of Life.* How to Have a Relationship With God. https://firelifeministries.org/firelife-ministries-blog/misplaced

'Life Without Father': Less College, Less Work, and More Prison for Young Men Growing Up Without Their Biological Father. (n.d.). Institute for Family Studies. https://ifstudies.org/blog/life-without-father-less-college-less-work-and-more-prison-for-young-men-growing-up-without-their-biological-father

Lowe, S. (2021, April 7). *Embracing Culture in the Blockbuster Film Season.* Finds.Life.Church. https://finds.life.church/blockbuster-film-season/

McMenamin, C. (2018, June 11). *God the Father: What it Means & 10 Example*. Crosswalk.com. https://www.crosswalk.com/faith/spiritual-life/10-ways-god-is-the-perfect-father-in-case-yours-wasn-t.html

Mellen, G. (2022, April 20). *Parents beware: Bullying, Pedophilia, Theft, Griefing, Doxing, Exploitation and Kill Stealing among on-line gaming risks*. Behind the Badge. Retrieved December 11, 2022, from https://behindthebadge.com/parents-beware-bullying-pedophilia-theft-griefing-doxing-exploitation-and-kill-stealing-among-on-line-gaming-risks/

Mentoring for Sons of Single Moms. (n.d.). Meier Clinics. https://www.meierclinics.com/mentoring-for-sons-of-single-moms/

Michelle, A. (2016, September 6). *5 Areas of Your Child's Life to Pray against Satanic Attack*. Crosswalk.com.

New American Standard Bible (NASB) - Version Information - BibleGateway.com. (n.d.). https://www.biblegateway.com/versions/New-American-Standard-Bible-NASB/

Noland, R. (2022, July). *"We'll Convert Your Children" – A Message from the San Francisco Gay Men's Choir*. Family Policy Alliance. Retrieved December 10, 2022, from https://familypolicyalliance.com/issues/2021/07/29/well-convert-your-children-a-message-from-the-san-francisco-gay-mens-choir/

Pincus, D. L., & Pincus, D. L. (2021, May 17). *When Parents Disagree: How to Parent as a Team*. Empowering Parents. https://www.empoweringparents.com/article/when-parents-disagree-how-to-parent-as-a-team/

Prayers For Deliverance From Demonic Attacks, Breaking Curses, And God's Protection. (2021, June 3). Jesus Truth Deliverance. https://jesustruthdeliverance.com/deliverance-from-demonic-attacks/

Quinn, M. (2022, August 2). *TikTokers Warn Each Other Not To Try Hypnosis Trend After Encountering 'Demonic' Figure While Under A Trance*. YourTango. https://www.yourtango.com/news/what-red-door-yellow-door-hypnosis-trend-tiktok

Raasch. (2018, September 16). *Are Parents Responsible for Their Children's Behavior? – Mount Olive Lutheran Church*. Mount Olive. Retrieved December 10, 2022, from https://www.mountoliveappleton.com/multimedia-archive/are-parents-responsible-for-their-childrens-behavior/

Rainey, D. and B. (2018, April 8). *Building Integrity Into the Life of Your Teen*. FamilyLife®. Retrieved December 11, 2022, from https://www.familylife.com/articles/topics/parenting/ages-and-stages/teens/building-integrity-into-the-life-of-your-teen/

Redbarnchurch. (2010, October 13). *Teaching Children to Choose Friends Wisely*. Christ Community Church. Retrieved December 10, 2022, from https://redbarnchurch.com/teaching-children-to-choose-friends-wisely/

Río, M. O. del. (2021, September 18). *Why didn't Steve Jobs let his kids use iPads?* mySA. https://www.mysanantonio.com/business/article/Why-didn-t-Steve-Jobs-let-his-kids-use-iPads-16468409.php

Rush, C. (2017, April). *Self-esteem: "I am not enough."* NexGen. Retrieved December 10, 2022, from https://www.premiernexgen.com/self-esteem-i-am-not-enough/11329.article

Saint James School of Medicine, Kralendijk, Bonaire, The Netherlands. (2013, April 3). *Maturation of the adolescent brain*. National Library of Medicine. Retrieved December 10, 2022, from https://www.ncbi.nlm.nih.gov/pmc/articles/PMC3621648/

Seaman, G. (2011, February). *7 Ways to Wean your Child off Video Games*. Eartheasy. Retrieved December 11, 2022, from https://learn.eartheasy.com/articles/7-ways-to-wean-your-child-off-video-games/

Sermonlink, P. (2022, January 6). *Parenting on Purpose*. pursueGOD.org. Retrieved December 11, 2022, from https://www.pursuegod.org/parenting-on-purpose/

Setupgamers. (2022, December 1). *13 Tragic Deaths Caused by Video Games*. Retrieved December 11, 2022, from https://www.setupgamers.com/deaths-caused-by-video-games/

Sherwood. (2022). *Off the Bench with Mark Sherwood*. *Heidi St. John The Busy Mom*. Retrieved December 5, 2022, from http://heidistjohn.com/blog/podcasts/offthebench-mark-sherwood

Smalley, G. &. M. (2004, March 15). *Life Support: Immediate Relationship Repair with Your Teen*. Crosswalk.com. https://www.crosswalk.com/family/parenting/life-support-immediate-relationship-repair-with-your-teen-1247815.html

Smith, J. (2018, March). *Kids Are Revealing What Their Parents Don't Know About Social Media & It's Disturbing*. Cafemom. Retrieved December 11, 2022, from https://cafemom.com/parenting/211190-parents-dont-know-social-media

Sorgius, K. (2022, November 1). *Work Unto the Lord: 10 Strategies to Teach Your Kids*. Not Consumed. https://www.notconsumed.com/work-unto-the-lord-10-strategies-to-teach-your-kids/

Stuckey, A. B. (2021). Ep 335 | Understanding the Biblical Telos of Gende. *Relatable with Allie Beth Stuckey*. Retrieved December 10, 2022, from https://podcasts.apple.com/us/podcast/ep-335-understanding-the-biblical-telos-of-gender/id1359249098?i=1000501589929

Sweet, J. (2022, March 24). *Tart Cherry Juice Is How Some Athletes Restore Their Body*. Sleep.com. https://www.sleep.com/sleep-health/tart-cherry-juice-benefits

Teach Kids About Money - Teach Kids How to Budget & Manage Money. (n.d.). https://thekingdomcode.com/about/teach-kids-about-money/

Teach Your Child How to Deal With a Bully. (2022, May 23). Verywell Family. https://www.verywellfamily.com/plan-for-standing-up-to-bullying-460810

Tennant, B. (2021, July 26). *The rod in Proverbs is not metaphorical*. Bnonn Tennant (the B Is Silent). https://bnonn.com/the-rod-in-proverbs-is-not-metaphorical/

The 4 Common Types of Bullying. (2022, June 3). Parents. https://www.parents.com/kids/problems/bullying/common-types-of-bullying/

The Magic Pajamas or 9 Ways To Help Kids Sleep Better According to Science. (2022, April 14). GoZen! https://gozen.com/9-ways-to-help-kids-sleep-better-according-to-science/

The Mama Bear Effect. (2022). Think All Child Molesters are Pedophiles? Think Again. *The Mama Bear Effect.* Retrieved December 10, 2022, from https://themamabeareffect.org/think-all-child-molesters-are-pedophiles-think-again/

Tumbokon, R. (2022, October). 25+ Positive & Negative Effects of Video Games, According to Science. *Raise Smart Kid.* Retrieved December 11, 2022, from https://www.raisesmartkid.com/3-to-6-years-old/4-articles/34-the-good-and-bad-effects-of-video-games

University Of Maryland School Of Medicine Study Shows Laughter Helps Blood Vessels Function Better. (n.d.). ScienceDaily. https://www.sciencedaily.com/releases/2005/03/050309111444.htm

Wang, S., Chen, L., Hailiang, R., Yusan, C., Fang, D., Sun, H., Peng, J., Liang, X., & Xiao, Y. (2022, August). *Depression and anxiety among children and adolescents pre and post COVID-19: A comparative meta-analysis.* National Library of Medicine. Retrieved December 11, 2022, from https://www.ncbi.nlm.nih.gov/pmc/articles/PMC9381924/

Wiesemann, D. (2020, October 22). *What Is the Armor of God for Kids in Simple Terms?* Children's Ministry Deals. https://www.childrens-ministry-deals.com/blogs/childrens-pastors-only/what-is-the-armor-of-god-for-kids-in-simple-terms

You Will NOT Believe How Satanic This New Video Game Is. (2022, August). [Video]. YouTube. Retrieved December 11, 2022, from

Wesley, J. (1766). A plain account of Christian perfection. World Invisible.

0Zapal, H. (2022, October 27). *How To Turn Off AirDrop and Keep Kids Safe.* Bark.

RESOURCES BOOK 2

The American Heritage® Dictionary of the English Language, Fifth Edition. (2022). In https://ahdictionary.com. Retrieved October 18, 2022, from https://ahdictionary.com/word/search.html?q=affirmation

New American Standard Bible. (2020) BibleGateway.com. https://www.biblegateway.com/passage/?search=Hebrews+4%3A12&version=NASB

Cahn, LC. (2021b, December 14). Celebrities Who Have Unusual Physical Traits. HealthDigest. Retrieved October 16, 2022, from https://www.healthdigest.com/676886/celebrities-who-have-unusual-physical-traits/

Ray Talks with Three Skater Girls. (2018, September 15). [Video]. YouTube. Retrieved October 16, 2022, from https://www.youtube.com/watch?v=Hw46OoSCc6g

Why I'm a Teenage Atheist. (2013, April 15). [Video]. YouTube. Retrieved October 16, 2022, from https://www.youtube.com/watch?v=yEB9yOtDrBM

Watts, A. (2019). An Easy Way to Teach Your Children to Think Before They Speak. iMom. Retrieved October 16, 2022, from https://www.imom.com/use-the-think-acronym/

Lisle, J. (2008, February 28). The Splendor of God's Creation. Answersingenesis.org. Retrieved October 16, 2022, from https://answersingenesis.org/astronomy/the-splendor-of-gods-creation/

Celebrate Every Day with Me. (2013, April 8). 25 Scripture Verses on Goal-Setting. Celebrate Every Day With Me. Retrieved October 16, 2022, from https://celebrateeverydaywithme.com/25-scripture-verses-on-goal-setting/

Gotquestions.org. (n.d.-b). What does it mean that God is Jehovah-Jireh? GotQuestions.org. Retrieved October 16, 2022, from https://www.gotquestions.org/Jehovah-Jireh.html

Bolinger, H. (2019, October 25). The Meaning Behind "Your Body is a Temple" & 5 Things You Should Be Doing. Crosswalk.com. Retrieved October 16, 2022, from https://www.crosswalk.com/faith/women/ways-to-treat-your-body-like-the-sacred-temple-it-is.html

Hall, A. (2013, April 26). Be Humble and Teachable to Lay the Foundation of Success. Forbes.com. Retrieved October 16, 2022, from https://www.forbes.com/sites/alanhall/2013/04/26/be-humble-and-teachable-to-lay-the-foundation-of-success/?sh=605e9ac66dda

Made in the USA
Columbia, SC
03 May 2023

0b6bb6d3-a541-4384-bfe2-4399a2d96d59R02